PARAMEDIC

PARAMEDIC

One woman's 20 years on the front line

SANDY MACKEN

ROCKPOOL
PUBLISHING

For Scarlett Rose

'*And now here is my secret, a very simple secret: it is only with the heart that one can see rightly; what is essential is invisible to the eye.*'
– Antoine de Saint-Exupéry, The Little Prince

'A miracle is a shift in perception from fear to love.'
– Marianne Williamson

To all of you who have helped this shift occur within me, and there are many. To every patient who grew my capacity for love and every colleague who stood by my side, this book is for you. For those of you who we've met and served and are looking for that spark of hope, and for the curious.

If not for the unending support of some really special people, this book would never have birthed. Dad for never doubting me or this work. My sisters for paving the way and calling me forward. Monica Crouch for your invaluable feedback, corrections, guidance and humour along the way. To my spiritual teacher Shakti Durga, for igniting my spirit and helping it grow so strong and bright. My hope is that this book helps to inspire people and open hearts. Last but certainly not least, I offer my work to beloved Sri Shakti Amma, to whom all of this belongs.

A Rockpool book
PO Box 252
Summer Hill
NSW 2130
Australia
www.rockpoolpublishing.com.au
www.facebook.com/RockpoolPublishing

First published in 2018
Copyright Text © Sandy Macken, 2018
Copyright Design © Rockpool Publishing, 2018

Cover, internal design and typesetting by Jessica Le, Rockpool Publishing
Edited by Lisa Macken

ISBN 978-1-925682-79-3
A catalogue record for this book is available from the National Library of Australia.

Printed and bound in China
10 9 8 7 6 5 4 3 2 1

In order to protect the privacy and identity of all, the names, dates and places of
events have been changed. The opinions expressed are the author's and do not
necessarily reflect the policy or position of any organisation she has worked for.
Since we are all critically thinking human beings, these views are always subject to
change, revision and rethinking at any time. Please do not hold the author to the
views expressed here, in perpetuity.

CONTENTS

INTRODUCTION

Look within. Within is the fountain of good, and it will ever bubble up if thou wilt ever dig. – Marcus Aurelius

I was fifteen years old the first time I saw ambulance paramedics working. They were known as 'ambos' then. I remember the wave of relief that came over me when they arrived only seconds later to help a man who had fallen over in the gutter. He had blood pouring from his face and I wanted so much for him to be okay. They were confident and quietly went about their business assisting him to his feet and cleaning his face. They were respectful, which I liked. There was something about seeing this old man dusted off and returned to his feet that made me feel so grateful they were there to help. It was an incredibly simple and yet inspiring moment that planted a seed that would gestate in the years to come.

More than ten years later I was that ambo, restoring calm to chaos and cleaning the streets of the fallen, wounded and unwell. At times I felt invincible, completely unaffected by life's trauma and tragedy, hungry for more experience to better my skill set and grow my bank of work experience in the field of pre-hospital care. I wore the uniform like a cape, with parts of me impenetrable.

My dad has always been a bit of a hero to me. An impressive man for many reasons – one being his decision to have another child, me, at the age of fifty despite the fact he already had ten children! The only downside to this is, of course, being advanced age, and when the time came to sit with him in the intensive care unit following major abdominal surgery, my superhero cape and every defence were stripped from me.

Convinced he was about to die and feeling completely helpless, I got to experience what it is like on the other side of health care. Now I was the terrified family member armed with a little bit of medical knowledge and irate at the lack of treatment being given. His heart rate thundered up to almost two hundred beats a minute, and I observed what I thought were his last moments in complete agony and despair.

Dad has no recollection of that event, one of the most distressing moments of my life, although he can recall with detail being given the choice to stay or to go.

As he recalled his time in near-death unconsciousness he told me: 'It was beautiful, Sand. I saw thousands of blue lights raining down and I knew they were blessings on us all. It was the most incredible thing I have ever seen.'

What I was doing at the same time was inwardly screaming at whatever god there was out there to get out of the clouds and help this man! When Dad told me of his experience, my whole world changed. I had a new set of glasses, and I knew that what we see with our eyes gives us a limited perspective. In the same moment I was in terror, Dad was in bliss.

Since then I have continued to see these two perspectives, the peace and the terror, or at the very least I have been aware that both are simultaneously possible. In every heartbreaking moment there is hope; with every death there is a dawn, and from every experience of being crushed there is opportunity to rise.

Paramedics are angels on earth, doing the dirtiest work there is to do. Most of their amazing work goes unnoticed, and you will never truly appreciate them for who they are unless you're on the receiving end of their care. Then you may have the grace to see their wings and feel the sense of gratitude that comes when your life, your safety and your comfort are held so well in their hands.

We are commonly asked: 'What's the worst thing you've seen?' We lie in response to that question, for our own sake as much as yours. We do see terrible things, but we also see inspiring things. We see the great capacity of the human spirit, the generosity of the human heart and the very good nature of most people.

We see the many cloaks that love and hope wear. We see these triumph again and again. We see hope dawn in the darkest nights and spring from barren wastelands. We bring peace to places from which it is absent, and we take home with us when the day is done a great sense of satisfaction. You see, the beauty and very good nature of the human spirit is everywhere, even in the terrible places.

So many people remark, 'I couldn't do your job, I can't stand blood.' For the record, I don't like blood either. I do my job for the love of it, for the love of life, the experience of hope and goodwill and the desire to be of service in the world. Yes, there is blood and sometimes plenty of it, but long gone are the days of chasing trauma. What really excites me now is experiencing the remarkable resilience of the human spirit.

I invite you to walk with me in my shoes. If we can find the peace and hope in these places, we can find it anywhere.

1

GROWING PAINS

And the day came when the risk to remain tight in a bud was more
painful than the risk it took to blossom. – Anais Nin

Some lessons come easy and some don't. Sometimes the line between
being a paramedic keen to treat sick patients and being a heartless,
arrogant twat gets a little blurred before we gain emotional maturity.
At some point in the first few years in the job I learned to rein in my
reaction to the 'big one', because a great day at work for me is often
the worst day in someone else's life.

We find ourselves in Sydney's Wentworth Street; it is mid-
morning. I'm a junior primary care paramedic and keen to get down
and dirty.

'Four-two-four thank you, you are responding to a hanging – no
further details as yet,' the dispatcher says in a stern monotone over
the airwaves. *Oh cool, I haven't done a hanging in a while, let's go, I*
think, as a wave of excitement rushes through me.

With smoking tyres, my partner Belinda and I hightail it to the
scene of this 'big' job. In ambo language, this equates to a 'good' job,
usually. We like the big jobs, the sicker the better, some say. It may
seem like a crazy mentality, but when we train for these events and

prepare ourselves it's the big jobs that test our skills. We get to see first-hand what all the studies and textbooks say about trauma, illness and injury; we get to enact our protocols and see the concrete effects of our treatment. It feels right, and even more right when there is a positive outcome. We wait for this work and spend countless hours preparing for it. It comes unexpectedly of course, when that call comes through: we might react with excitement for all these reasons. We're not sickos; it's just how we're wired.

For now I'm green enough to be hungry for big jobs, a hunger that peters out over time for many ambos as the psyche fills up with so much sadness that any more might make you burst and leave a mess too big to clean up.

As we jump the median strip and weave our way through King Street in Newtown, Belinda is herding the traffic like sheep. It's the closest either of us will come to country life and we laugh out loud at the frantic dash people make to clear a path for us. I lazily pull on a pair of our unmistakable blue gloves as Belinda navigates her way through the back streets.

'Do you want me to look it up?' I offer, already opening the famous Gregory's street directory. The heavy workload in this area is obvious – the pages for Newtown are tattered and marked with notes by other ambos. There are circles marking regular addresses and the occasional skull or cross.

When I trained, map reading was a vitally important skill – and a huge source of anxiety when working outside the normal catchment area. It wouldn't be unusual to see an ambo steering the truck with one hand while juggling the Gregory's in the other. We'd write frantic notes on the back of latex gloves, indicating how many streets to pass before turning right, then left, then the second exit at the roundabout before travelling a further kilometre, my goodness, and so on. This was how we tracked down the sick and injured.

These days we have the luxury of GPS, and just about every smartphone has a voice-activated map navigator. Navigation systems are also built into the ambulance. What a relief it is to set out knowing we're headed in the right direction on the quickest route to our patient without the added stress of having to refer to the street directory.

'No thanks, mate, this address is right near my place, I can get us there,' Belinda replies. That's never a good thing; one always ponders the possibility that an address near home will involve a neighbour or friend. We've all heard the stories, the unbelievable nightmare of treating your own family. *I hope this isn't anybody we know*, I think, and with that thought my excitement eases to moderate anticipation. I am still stoked to be on this job, but maybe I'm not punching the air.

In all of seven minutes we pull in for a tidy approach and I remark, 'Nice parking, sister!' as we step out of the car in perfect unison. We're greeted by the familiar smell of burning brakes and the unfamiliar sound of flowerpots being launched from an upper storey balcony. Distinct cries of terror and grief echo around the buildings, which stand as icy witnesses to the day's events. The screaming and smashing pots indicate we're in the right place and that it shouldn't be too difficult to locate the patient. Like a magnet, it draws us closer.

'Okay, so we're up there, I suppose,' I say. *I hope they can buzz us in*, I think, completely absorbed in the logistics of getting to a higher floor in an apartment building.

The gear feels weightless as we stride up three flights of stairs. We know it's a hanging but we still don't know the state of the patient, which means all the gear comes with us. A twelve kilogram vinyl backpack known as an Oxy-Viva comes with us; it's complete with an oxygen cylinder plus every type of oxygen mask we use and a cardiac monitor and defibrillator, known as the Lifepak, in case the patient is in cardiac arrest (often futile really, due to the fact that the patient's brain has been starved of oxygen long enough to cause cardiac arrest; we can often restart the heart but we will never save that brain). Then there's a relatively lightweight bag containing at least five or six cervical collars that provide a rigid support to the neck if we suspect it's broken, which we always do in a hanging. There's a drug kit that's like a large suitcase and also weighing in at about twelve kilograms, and a spineboard that looks like a large, flat surfboard to keep the patient flat in cases of suspected spinal injury. It all comes with us to the patient.

I want to take the stairs two at a time but I control the internal urgency and take a steady walk to the apartment. My partner is right behind me. I'm the treating officer today and the intensive care paramedics are a long way off. By that I mean ten to fifteen minutes, which can seem like eternity when you're out of your depth.

With one more flight to go, the screaming becomes more intense. *It's too early and too cold to be breaking a sweat*, I think. *Why is it always up the top?* I think to myself as I walk as quickly as possible with the gear to the patient.

'This way, ambos!' a police officer calls to us as he strides ahead and leads the way up the stairs. We are just a bit slower on our feet; it might be the forty-odd kilos of equipment we're carrying, or the fact that at the time we're both heavy smokers. I'll blame it on the equipment: it's bulky and cumbersome, a fact almost every greeter at a scene overlooks.

Apparently everyone is oblivious to the hysterical young woman who seems to be having some sort of psychotic episode on the balcony. I don't get a chance to check for epaulettes on the shoulder of his uniform, so I cannot tell if our greeting police officer is fresh or not.

Like us, police personnel wear their rank on their shoulders. You can tell if a police officer, affectionately known as a 'cop', is senior or junior by the number of lines they wear on this part of their uniform. Ambos also wear rank, both clinical and management related. It helps to know the level of seniority in police and ambos at a glance. To wear certain rank, you need time in the job, experience and competence. A sense of relief comes with the presence of high-ranking clinical professionals on a job – there's relief in the presence of someone who knows what they're doing, and can take control and make good decisions.

On this particular day the epaulettes on my shoulders indicate I'm qualified to do this job unsupervised but I'm not senior by any stretch. I am not 'green' or new, but I am years away from earning the respected title of 'frog' – intensive care paramedic. It's a funny term, really, apparently used because 'everyone they touched croaked', but we use it as a term of great respect. Most of us hope to earn that title one day, and I am frequently in awe of the frogs I work alongside. They are always so calm and seem to know exactly what to do in every circumstance.

Rank or no rank, the cop is looking wide-eyed and neither he nor anyone else is doing anything to stop the woman from throwing pots over the balcony. They continue to smash and for a second I consider my helmet, which is still in the truck. How ridiculous that would look, but I still think about the vulnerability of my skull and I'm a bit pissed off that the cop isn't managing this crazy behaviour.

Do you think one of you guys could control that lady? I think, becoming a tad concerned about the increasing hysteria. This thought must be written all over my face as I gaze in the direction of the noise with a furrowed brow.

'That's the girlfriend,' the officer says, guiding us into the scene. 'She found him hanging in the stairwell inside. I think he's gone.'

At this point my mind tunes the screaming woman out of focus. Her emotions are spewing out all over the place, which is understandable, but if this guy needs us to work on him it's best if we're not distracted. The mind takes a single track: all we want is access to the patient.

The first thing I see as I walk though the apartment door is a cop with a notebook in hand looking relieved to see us. We're in a lounge room that has a lived-in feel, a little cluttered perhaps – these people are not from the upper end of the socio-economic spectrum – but it's homely, and the officer looks out of place standing in the middle of the lounge room. There is carpet and a print of an eagle on the wall. The air isn't thick with cigarette smoke as in many public housing units, and there are DVDs piled up on the coffee table. Then I see him. Not hanging, but lying on the couch. He's not sleeping, though; he's most certainly dead.

At first glance my mind plays a trick and I think for a second he's been eating a blue snake. *Maybe he vomited it up, or choked on this blue snake?* A second later my mind corrects itself and I realise the snake I am seeing is his tongue. It's way too long and it's stuck, as if frozen, out of his mouth.

'He was hanging by his belt. The girlfriend cut him down and put him on the sofa here,' the officer informs us. It feels like awkward small talk loaded with expectation, and yet I'm already starting to feel out of my depth, like I don't quite know what to say.

'Um, righteo then,' I say, a little scared to touch the body but curious to know if it's cold.

This is not looking good, he is blue, cold, he looks dead, he has no movement, he must have been here a while, I think, as my brain moves out of treatment mode and into scene management. After what feels like ages but is probably only a few seconds I have my next thought: *confirm the obvious and call it in on the radio. He's dead.*

Even though everyone in the room suspects and even knows this guy is dead, they wait and watch the ambos go through the motions and say the words. We put the ECG leads on and press our record button on the Lifepak machine. We let the printer run off a strip of ECG paper. Out it comes: a perfectly flat line, absolutely nothing going on in the heart, just as we all suspected.

'Four-two-four, patient is deceased,' I say into the portable radio microphone that sits on my shoulder.

Up to this point it's all pretty much science. If we can get in there and out in less than ten minutes, the psyche doesn't seem to take in the horror. The uncontained emotions of the loved ones who found the body can almost bounce off us; we can acknowledge how tragic the job was, and move on to the next one relatively unscathed.

If, however, circumstances dictate that we stay longer on the scene, then another story begins to unfold. We learn about the characters involved in the tragedy; we learn the name of the departed and the names of the neighbours and we hear about how they met and who they are. It is no longer science, but a real-life story of which we are a part. It becomes our real-life story too.

I am still in the scientific phase, taking note of the fact this young man was in good shape and is wearing designer underwear. There is a very strange juxtaposition as his body lies on the couch: his lower half looks like a Calvin Klein model, but his head tells a very different story. His face, contorted in a freeze frame at the moment of death, is icy blue. He is lying here as I imagined he might do when kicking back with his girlfriend watching TV, but with his jarring blue tongue.

I lift my head as I again tune in to the sound of pots being thrown from the balcony. 'He's gone! I love him!' echoes around the buildings. Then in through the front door comes a woman, and I know instinctively this is his mother. There is something about her gaze and singleness of purpose that says this to me. She doesn't seem to notice anything at all accept his body on the couch.

Fuck, how am I going to say this? I think, as an electric shock of panic runs through me and hits my toes. I know it is my job to tell her: this man, her son, is dead. Sometimes people don't realise what is obvious to us, and need to be told quite directly that someone is deceased. It is never an easy conversation and I am already scratching my mind for the words.

She doesn't see the six police officers standing outside the apartment, and she doesn't see me, despite the fact I'm sitting right next to her son. She doesn't flinch at the sound of the pots smashing. She makes a direct line for the patient just as we did, only this is her son, her own flesh and blood, who lies here dead.

Hmm, we're stuck here for a while now, I think. *The girlfriend is demented with grief and will probably need to be transported to hospital. Mum is going to need some support and an explanation. I wonder if she knows what happened.*

Some ambos have the gift of the gab, and up until this very day I thought that included me. After a few years' experience I usually know what to say and how to say it. I thought I knew how to sound professional and polite yet caring and sensitive, and how to prepare a person for the procedures following a death. I thought I knew it all. Until this very moment, I thought I knew it all.

I had built walls around my heart and led with my head. Arrogant and self-assured, I had walked myself into a barren wasteland without knowing it, and my mental resources were now failing me utterly. I feel useless, paralysed.

The mother sits on a coffee table next to the sofa and faces her son. The sounds of pots shattering outside continues in stark contrast to Mum's quiet composure. It's confronting.

Um, should I say something here? I think. *She does know he's dead, doesn't she? What the fuck do I say? Are they waiting for me to speak?*

I exchange a glance with Belinda, who stares back at me and gives a quick shoulder shrug; she clearly has nothing to add. Apparently I'm not the only one feeling stuck. I want desperately to offer something but have nothing of worth. I have no words.

'Oh, my darling baby boy, I didn't know, I never knew. Honey, why didn't you tell me you were so depressed?' she asks him. She cradles his face in her loving arms and doesn't even flinch at his contorted expression, his stare into space. She doesn't seem to see any of that. She continues with her terribly beautiful monologue, and she is completely composed as she speaks to him.

'Darling, darling boy. My sweet boy, all you had to do was say something. How could I know you were so sad? My little angel darling boy, all the love in the world is here for you. I have always loved you, my sweet. I know things were tough last year, and I know you've been smoking, your mother knows everything about you. I've never stopped loving you, sweetheart. I never will stop loving you. Why didn't you let me know how much you were suffering, sweet, sweet, boy?'

She speaks with such tenderness, her mother's love completely unbound. I wish he were still alive to hear this. If only he were not so dead.

As for me, who only half an hour ago was remarking how 'cool' it was because we hadn't done a hanging in a while, I'm completely stumped. I sit on the coffee table with Mum right next me and I rest my hand on her back. I'm mute, her silent witness, deeply humbled in this moment. Now it is me who is frozen; for the first time in my life I have no words. Not a single word comes to me so I can't form even the simplest sentence to offer support. I'm shell-shocked; I have nothing.

As I sit frozen in this parent's worst nightmare, Mum starts singing a lullaby to her son.

'Day is done, gone the sun from the lake, from the hills, from the sky … all is well, safely rest,' she sings. She caresses him and rocks him back and forth, and quietly, gently sings to him.

Oh my God, this is awful, should the cops get her details? Um, I should tell her there's nothing we can do. We tried. No, we didn't. Do I say 'I'm sorry'? Do I ask if he suffered from depression? Did anyone know? Do I speak now? Are they waiting for me? Why is nobody speaking?

Now I'm aware of my chest; it feels like my organs are pierced with hooks that are pulling me heavily towards the earth. My throat aches. Still I have no words as my hand rests on Mum's back, trying pathetically to support this woman somehow as she sings to her dead son.

I should say something. What do I say? Still I have no words. *I need support here! Come on, guys, help me out here.* I glance at Belinda, who is busying herself with her glasses, and I catch the eye of the cop standing at the other end of the room next to her partner. All I see is their glistening cheeks as tears stream from everyone in the room.

Mum sings to her son and her love hits my heart like a furnace to ice. The effect is immediate. As the ice melts my eyes become flood gates, and behind them the dams are about to burst.

I am so sorry, I think. I am so sorry, for the excitement I felt at the thought of this job. I am so sorry that your son can't hear you right now, I am so sorry that I don't know what to say, I am so sorry for your loss. I am so sorry that he saw no other way out, that he felt so alone. I am so sorry for the girlfriend, that she's alone now. I am so sorry. I am so sorry that there is nothing I can do, that I have no words right now.

But none of these words leave my lips. Instead, my mouth is fixed ever so slightly ajar and sadness furrows my brow. It is seconds only but it feels like an eternity as love enters my world once again, tearing me apart in a terrible but necessary way.

This is fucked. My partner and the police have no words either. 'I'm going to take some of the equipment downstairs, back in a minute,' I say to Belinda.

I stand and feel dizzy. The sound of the cracking pots seems dampened and distant. I feel as if I am in a bubble, not sure if I'm going to throw up, faint or cry. I can't tell; my body feels strange. I see the open door and walk towards it, down the stairs and into the sunlight on the street. I feel the fresh air. The sweet relief of leaving that space hits me like a ray of sunshine on a cold winter's morning.

It's just me now; I'm safe to just be me again. The flood gates open and I burst into tears, sobbing in the sun, feeling like a failure. It's like I'm vomiting emotion into the gutter, I cannot hold this in a moment longer. I want to stop myself but I can't. Tears of frustration, that there is nothing we can do, tears about God knows what, and snot – lots of snot. I grab a handful of tissues and blow this job out of my brain and into the tissue. I stifle the rest of my tears as quickly as I can, scared that someone will see me. Scared that I'm a failure, that I'm weak, that I've let the team down, that I can't handle the job. Then I suck it all in as quickly as possible, wipe the fog from my sunglasses and take a deep breath.

I exhale. After I've thrown the gear into the back of the truck, I reach straight for my cigarettes and spark one up: a deep inhale and long exhale. I can't quite make out how many neighbours are making a nuisance of themselves trying to take a look at this fiasco, as my tears are still pooling in my lower lids and everything is a blur. I rest my back against the warm side door of the ambulance and once again the ache in my throat reminds me of just how very human I am.

There are dangers in this work, an obvious one in this case being the flying and smashing pots. There would have been a nasty wound if one had struck my head, but it was easy to see and therefore easy to avoid. It would also be easy to treat.

Another terracotta pot smashes to the ground as an incoherent scream echoes around cold brick walls. *For fuck's sake, restrain that woman!* I yell internally, as I slowly exhale a lungful of soothing, nicotine-enriched goodness. Never again will I get excited about a 'big job'. Deeply humbled, I'm reminded that I'm a member of the human race first and an ambo second. Perhaps the most valuable humbling sinks in at a deep level: the line is so fine, it shifts unpredictably.

Eventually the pot-throwing woman becomes my patient, and I hear many stories of the love between her and the man who has died: how they met, their secret engagement and plans to elope. I hear some details about the family and the pressures of a cross-cultural relationship. I hear what she loves about him and what she hates. I hear her frustration, how she felt when he smoked drugs and shut her out. That she is scared and angry, has no idea how to live without him and blames him. I hear about how confused she is that she could love someone so much who has left her behind with such a mess.

'Love is like that sometimes,' I manage to say. Mostly I listen, as we drive her up to the emergency department at her request. Perhaps she thinks there is a solution up there. At least there will be people to talk to.

A deep passion for being of service to others drives my love of the job, yet this job is dealing with life and death. The two cannot be separated, and I need to reconcile them within. It takes a certain type of person to love this work when it means repeated and prolonged exposure to tragedy and death. To deny the emotions feels unnatural, but we must always be professional and strong. Sometimes the work cuts straight to the heart and our professional demeanour or apparent heartless exterior is shattered in a single glance.

As ambos, our capacity to hold this space for others grows along with our medical knowledge. We fumble our way through, like the rest of humanity. Our hearts grow, our capacity to hold the lightness and the depth of the human experience expands and matures. These are the growing pains of the huge paramedic heart. In the early years, the best I could do was suck those ciggies all the way down to the butt, swallow the lumps in my throat and soldier on to the next case. I'd say 'I'm fine' when probably I wasn't.

To live life with a closed heart robs us of our connection to humanity, and without that connection we are alone. There is no greater burden than that. It is through the heart that we allow others to share the load. I had been walking alone without knowing it and was guided back to my heart by the unconditional love of the mother. I had no idea how hungry for love I was, but in order to be fed I would need to feel.

There would come a time years later, when drinking would no

longer work and the ciggies were long gone, that the unconditional love of the mother-divine would save me once again, would navigate me away from the wastelands of a closed heart and home to love once more. In hindsight I can see that this force of love trickles through the miasma of life like a river in search of the ocean, and I am both river and ocean. Try as I may to outrun this force of nature it finds me every time, and with each encounter I am restored.

My love for the job builds my capacity for love of people. The pain builds my capacity for compassion, and these growing pains, these so-called 'failures', will become the very fabric of which this tapestry of love is woven. Only in hindsight and after many years do I realise this. For now, it's just another job, another reason to smoke, to drink after work, and another story to not tell.

2

HOPE SPRINGS

Hope begins in the dark, the stubborn hope that if you just show up and try to do the right thing, the dawn will come. You wait and watch and work: you don't give up. – Anne Lamott

Methodically I go through the motions of cleaning up at hospital. The previous job was so unremarkable I can't recall the patient's name and, quite frankly, that's okay. I remove dirty linen and throw it in the linen skip in the emergency department. I wash down the waterproof coating on the stretcher, then take the clean, folded sheet and fling it out over the stretcher with all the accuracy of a casino croupier. I fold each corner of the crispy white sheet perfectly around the corners of the ambulance stretcher. *Why can't I be this perfectionist with my own bedroom?* I ponder as I remember the state in which I left my room this morning.

It's not unusual to find a paramedic a little preoccupied with detail from time to time. The desire for perfection, or at least the capacity for self-assessment and constant improvement, is a trait I see in many colleagues. I place myself in that category too. There is something deeply satisfying about knowing no matter how hard you tried, you could not have done that job better. Every job offers an opportunity for self-reflection and growth. In my early years these high expectations caused me a great degree of stress, the blame seeming to rest so easily on my own shoulders. With time I came to believe that I am really a small piece in a much larger puzzle than I at first appreciated. Sometimes our best performance as paramedics still results in death, and sometimes people survive against impossible odds. My role is to do my best in every moment, and trust that the universe will make the big decisions about life and death.

I love working on Saturdays: everyone else is enjoying their day off and the city's vibe changes. The streets are relatively quiet, as the working population deals with the hangover earned from Friday night drinks. The sports ovals smell like freshly cut lawn and somewhere off in the distance I can hear a whistle blowing on a football field. I love that sound; it reminds me of my childhood, the years I lived on the grounds of one of Sydney's most prestigious high schools. The memory takes me back to those fun, warm, innocent times, riding the bike with training wheels, kicking balls around and generally enjoying the riches of my childhood.

Footy injuries will start soon, I think, as I rest my upper body on my freshly made stretcher and watch another ambulance reverse into the vehicle bay at Royal Prince Alfred hospital. My colleague Amanda is completing her paperwork. Well, that's what she should be doing, since we just offloaded our patient. She mentioned something about coffee after this job and I'm pretty happy with that plan. One of those unwritten rules in our job is that the person on overtime rates pays for the coffee, and Amanda is working overtime today. It's always a bit of a lottery when your partner calls in sick and leaves you single on the roster for the day, because that's when they call in someone on overtime. I feel lucky today. Amanda was in my induction class six years ago; she is familiar and lovely. With the same amount of time in the service, we can pretty much know how to run any job without having to keep an eye on each other. She's clever, too. Recently she completed her intensive care course, which means she is clinically senior to me and will be taking responsibility for any big work that we do today. At the start of the shift she mentions this is her first overtime shift as an intensive care paramedic. It's a big deal and I imagine a bit stressful, as this will be the first time she's worked with someone of a junior clinical rank.

'I am glad I am working with you, mate. At least one of us knows our way around the city,' Amanda says, placing the case sheet folder on the dash.

'That's for sure. It's always fun and games in the city,' I reply, simultaneously collapsing the front wheels and sliding the stretcher into the locking mechanism. I'm the driver today, which means I don't shoulder the heavy clinical responsibility. I feel relaxed working alongside an intensive care paramedic; their extra training is always evident, and the big decisions will rest with Amanda today. It's my job to support her, drive to jobs, assist with clinical skills when needed and drive the ambulance to hospital.

'Nine-eighty-four. Nine-eighty-four for a casualty call please. Nine-eighty-four, can you clear?'

Must be a big job, the dispatcher either has the shits or he needs us, I think, as I move promptly in the direction of the radio. It is the tone in his voice, the way he says, 'can you clear' that evokes my quick response.

I lean over the front seat and grab hold of the microphone.

'Eighty-four, we're just finishing the cleaning, we can clear,' I state as I gesture to my partner that we will have to head off. Amanda is finishing a conversation with another paramedic as the details come over the air to us from a dispatcher who sounds very focused.

'Nine-eighty-four, thank you. You are heading to Maroubra for a toddler of unknown age who is query code two, address to follow, over.'

Righteo, toddler in cardiac arrest. Crap! I think before my mind jumps into gear and begins some supportive and calming inner dialogue.

We've done the training, we know what to do. Amanda is treating today and I am the assistant. Still, my heart jumps when I hear the job details. Even we paramedics are hungry for 'good' work, but when it involves a child who is critically ill it's *never* good. We all know the statistics: if they're very young and in cardiac arrest, the odds of survival are low at best. The only real hope we have is that the information could be incorrect; maybe the child has had a seizure. In any case, I'm flooded with dread.

Amanda steps up into the ambulance, and I have the wheels rolling before the door is closed. I know the distance we have to travel and I'm very concerned. Saturday traffic can be a nightmare, and we need to get through the city to the eastern suburbs fast.

Thank God I'm driving! I think; I know every shortcut. I also know where the traffic tends to get congested at this time on a Saturday. Usually I would wait till we reach the end of the street before turning the siren on, but not this time. I'm hanging a hard right turn with lights and siren blazing just seconds after receiving the call.

'Mate, I can get us close to the address then I'll need you to look up the exact location for me,' I say as I flash the car in front and swerve around in a fluid motion.

'Yes, okay. I have to get the drug doses right. I'll need some time to work out the math. Point one of a mil per kilo. Do we have an age?'

'Not as yet. He just said toddler.'

'Nine-eighty-four,' Amanda says into the radio.

'Nine-eighty-four?' the radio responds.

'Thanks, just wondering if you could get on the call back and get us the weight of the child?' she says, with the sirens blazing in the background.

'Copy nine-eighty-four, I'll see what we can do.'

I am totally focused and I'm not shy with the accelerator. I sit in the outside lane mostly. It's important never to allow the vehicle to get boxed in. We can jump the median strip when we need to, and I frequently cross over into oncoming traffic and steer cars out of our way. Every set of lights seems to be green; it's like Moses himself is parting the sea of traffic for us. I navigate our way through the inner city in less than five minutes, straight through a green-light corridor.

So far, so good, I think as we fly through the streets. Amanda is writing numbers on her blue glove and her body sways as I swerve through the traffic. She is completely trusting of my driving; either that, or she's shitting herself over the job. I don't envy her.

Within an unbelievably short time we're in the general vicinity of the job. It has been the smoothest traffic flow I think I have ever seen in the city. Sometimes it is so clear that the gods are on our side.

'Okay, Mands, I need you to look up the address, mate.'

'Are we nearly there?' she responds, a little flustered at having been interrupted. There are so many mental notes to make before these cases and so little time to prepare. Once we work out the drug doses it becomes much easier, but we need the time to calculate. Amanda has notes on her gloves, which will come in useful, but if she doesn't start directing me we won't have our patient in front of us.

Amanda looks up for the first time in minutes and sees we're nearly in Maroubra. I get a sense of her anxiety and I feel a little excited too, even slightly nauseated; my palms are sweating and my mind is moving fast. Conscious of my breathing, I mindfully exhale long, full breaths to calm myself before we arrive.

'This is my first paediatric arrest. I'm glad we're working together,' Amanda says.

Me too! I think, safe in the knowledge Amanda is a more than capable paramedic. We have trained together over the years and it's a good feeling, knowing you can trust your partner.

'We'll be fine. You've got your drug doses, just tell me what you want. You know your stuff. Deep breaths, mate, I just really need some directions now, or I'm afraid we'll get lost!'

'Yep, Okay. Let's see. Take a left here. Second street on your right is a laneway.'

I throw the truck around the corner and see what looks like a man standing on the corner waving his arms frantically. *How'd he know we were coming this way?* I wonder, knowing this is one of at least three possible approaches to the house.

The man indicates we should head down the laneway. At the next corner is the same thing, a woman this time standing with her arms in the air.

Sheesh, they're all over this! Usually the 'wavers' stand out the front of the address and wave us down, but today there are people three blocks away from the address signalling us in. There is a real sense of intensity and urgency. I'm grateful for their forward thinking and quietly relieved that we chose the best way to get to the address.

It has now been nine minutes from the time we received the call and we've travelled about fifteen kilometres. It's nothing short of a miracle that we got here so quickly.

It doesn't really matter how much time we have before we enter a scene like this; what matters is that we have *some* time. There are lots of things that need to take place to get us here, like map reading, negotiating the traffic, confirming drug doses and a brief plan of attack. Perhaps the most important processes we go through, mental preparation and focus, are for most paramedics subconscious. We have enough information to know we are about to walk into a devastating and highly emotional scene. It's our job to anticipate this, then compose ourselves and work effectively.

There is already an ambulance at the address. This is typical for such cases, as it takes a minimum of two crews to manage the task. A supervisor would usually be dispatched as well. There can be difficult issues to address, such as the welfare of parents, the occasional obstruction and unhelpful input from bystanders as well as their safety and psychological well-being. And, of course, our fellow paramedics, who also need support and assistance to create a safe and spacious working environment. Supervisors are great for that; they're clinicians as well, which means they have all the training we do and can treat a patient if necessary. However, their real role on these jobs is watching our backs and looking after the peripheral workload.

On jobs like this there is usually a cast of thousands and today is no exception. Mostly people are standing still; some have their hands over their mouths, some are pale, and they all look serious.

I bring the truck to an abrupt stop, strategically placing us alongside the ambulance crew that is already working on a small child, who lies completely lifeless on the grass beside the footpath. He is waxy white, and he looks dead.

The seatbelt is released and I open the door in one fluid movement. As I step out of the ambulance I smell the distinct odour of burning brakes.

I hope they're not smoking, I think, as I remember an incident some months ago involving a colleague, burning brakes, a fire and a fire extinguisher. There are no flames, thankfully, and I refocus quickly as I stride with Amanda toward the child.

We are in the back streets of suburban Maroubra. I glance around to see what we are walking into. The street is a cul-de-sac with no through traffic, which is a good thing. Big crowds and traffic congestion, as well as noise, can be distracting. There must be close to fifteen people standing silently around. All eyes are glued on us as we approach.

The child is laid out on the nature strip next to the footpath. The houses look warm and inviting, and the area seems affluent. It's the kind of street kids would play cricket in, with lots of picket fences, and I catch a glimpse of a rose bush in full bloom. Someone has been taking good care of the garden.

The child's little body is so white. Lifeless. I can see he is dead.

There are three defined circles around the child. The first one contains two people, two primary care paramedics. I recognise the male, and see that the other, a young woman, is a trainee. She is performing external cardiac massage on the child and counting aloud.

'Two, three, four, five,' she counts as she pumps the small, lifeless chest. The senior of the two, the male I recognise, is holding a resuscitator mask over the child's face. I can see there is an oral airway in the child's mouth. The piece of plastic at the child's lips is baby blue. The curved plastic oral airway sits at the back of the tongue, holding it in place so the child can be artificially ventilated, a process that involves blowing oxygen into his lungs by squeezing a resuscitator bag.

Oh God, no, this is bad, I think. It's more a wave of emotion than a coherent thought.

The next circle comprises two people. I know instantly that the woman standing behind the airway paramedic is the mother; I can see it in her eyes. There is another person standing to the left of the mother and I assume this is a neighbour. They watch wide-eyed the horror unfolding on the footpath.

About twenty metres away stands the rest of the neighbourhood, all looking silently horrified as we move in to treat the patient.

His little body is limp, all white with arms slightly splayed out to the side. He's wearing a nappy and his tiny body is exposed. It's not a warm day, and I assume the paramedics have cut off his clothes. My instincts register the temperature and the fact he is not clothed, and I want so terribly to think along the lines of 'poor little darling looks cold' but I cannot allow myself that thought. At this stage, he is clinically dead. There are no signs of life and the cardiac monitor shows the heart is completely devoid of electrical activity.

It's difficult to ignore the feelings in my body: my chest feels heavy, my throat tightens a little. There is absolutely *nothing* good about this job. It feels like there has been a terrible mistake that we need to correct. We *have to* give him another chance! We experience this intensity and urgency internally while outwardly we remain focused, diligent and calm. We all have a role to play in this resuscitation, and each part needs to be performed well if we are to gain a positive outcome.

The chest compressions and oxygen feed are good. The next steps are to implement more advanced resuscitation, which requires more invasive access to his respiratory and cardiac systems, so Amanda and I step into that role. She will intubate the child and I will attempt to gain intravenous access.

I open the drug bag and pull out a small cannula. At Amanda's request I attempt to get intravenous access, sliding the cannula into the crook of his little elbow. Nothing; he is too shut down. I cannot even see his veins. I can guess where to go but there is literally nothing. I search everywhere: his arms, hands, neck and feet. I know this is not going to work, that he needs the needle that goes straight into the bone, but I'm not qualified to do this so Amanda will have to attempt it later. If she gets the tube into his lungs, at least we can administer drugs down the tube.

It's not ideal, but one of the problems that tend to arise. It makes me feel hopeless and a little useless. I just wish I could find a vein. If we had access to his veins with this cannula I'm holding, we could start feeding adrenaline into his system and possibly excite and activate the heart. I plunge the sharp needle into the crook of his other elbow – another failed attempt.

One of the other crew members gives us a handover as we work, after the immediate tasks have been established.

'Okay, guys, he is thirteen months old. Apparently Mum found him floating face down in their play pool. She did CPR immediately and we took over. Total down time so far is about twelve minutes. He is currently being monitored in asystole. So far we've seen no response from the compressions,' he says. It makes such a difference when people are calm, and to his credit he is clear and cool. We all interpret the medical jargon, and it is about as bad as it could get.

'Asystole' refers to the rhythm of the heart, that dreaded flat line you've seen on TV when someone dies. We like to see at least a little bit of a squiggly line, as it means there is still some electrical activity going on and a patient will sometimes respond to the drugs we give in such cases. A straight flat line in a child is the worst possible thing to see.

Oh no, this is so bad. Does Mum have any idea how bad the prognosis is? I wonder.

The four of us are working on the child in a tight circle; we all have our defined roles. We know the statistics, and I don't think anyone present believes this child will survive. Of course, this doesn't change our treatment; we give it everything we've got. The job is running smoothly and Amanda directs us all to a task.

Mum stands at the head of the patient looking horrified. She has vomit on her face, which I assume gurgled up and out of her son's stomach as she performed mouth to mouth. She seems oblivious to the vomit and looks as though she's in a trance. She is unbelievably calm, and paramedics are always grateful for that. The job is hard enough to get through and often harder when bystanders are yelling or frantic, even though it would be understandable if they were.

We spend all of four minutes on scene inserting an endotracheal (ET) tube into the child. Amanda commences the first dose of adrenaline and we make moves for the ambulance. She has had to administer the adrenaline down the tube and into the child's lungs, and although this is a valid route of administration I feel like a failure for not being able to cannulate him. We all work in unison to roll our little patient onto a spineboard so we can carry him to the stretcher that awaits.

We maintain cardiopulmonary resuscitation throughout, knowing that if we stop this for even a few seconds the boy will be deprived of oxygen and become brain damaged. My chest is heavy with emotion, but I force the dread and anxiety down so I can remain focused. I will my feelings away and continue to make quick decisions to keep the job moving along. It appears that everyone else is doing the same.

It's my job to prepare the back of the ambulance, so I help load the stretcher then jump into the driver's seat. The other ambulance crew climbs in the back with Amanda, so travelling in the back of the ambulance we have the patient on the stretcher, Amanda on the treat seat next to him, a paramedic seated in the airway seat at the patient's head and a supervisor standing in the space between them. At this stage the supervisor will continue the chest compressions as the other two ambos take care of the ventilations and the drug regime. The mother is being transported to hospital in a police car, and I as the driver am being directed to follow another police car; we're getting a police escort. There is some relief that comes with having the job contained within the back of the vehicle, as we can now talk frankly as a team.

Righteo, God, safe passage please, get us there swiftly, I silently pray before taking off slowly. 'You guys have ten minutes or so between here and hospital,' I call out.

'Righteo, mate,' Amanda responds.

Treatment continues as we drive under lights and sirens smoothly to hospital. It is imperative that the treatment in the back is uninterrupted, so my driving is swift yet steady. The police car darts ahead and stops traffic at each intersection so we can drive through. The lights and siren are on, but I am travelling at normal speed to avoid throwing my colleagues around too much and I take the corners slowly.

'So, do you think the mum's compressions were effective?' Amanda asks.

'Oh yeah, she was doing a great job. She said it could only have been three minutes maximum before she found him,' Mark, one of the other crew members, says.

'How did it happen?' Amanda asks again as she draws up another dose of adrenaline.

'Well, yesterday he couldn't unlock the gate, but today he could. He lifted the latch, crawled over and tipped himself in.'

No way! How terrible! I think.

'The mum had just done a first aid course last week though,' Mark remarks as he maintains compressions.

'Seven, eight, nine, ten,' he calls aloud to indicate how many compressions he has performed and when the next breath is indicated.

Mark pauses compressions ever so slightly as the resuscitation bag is squeezed and another breath is delivered to the clinically dead boy. My eyes dart between the road and rear-vision mirror, watching as much as I can of what is happening in the back so I can time the corners well.

It is a quick trip to hospital and I have notified them of our pending arrival via a radio message. Every ambo in the area would have tuned in to that report, and everyone's heart would have sunk. The statistics are far from favourable for a child in cardiac arrest. It feels like there is no hope.

We pull into the hospital driveway feeling grim. We were unable to gain access to the boy's veins with a cannula, and there is no needle into his bone. All the drugs have gone into his lungs, and I think this will mean the end for him. I'm already sinking with guilt. Our little boy is still waxy white with no signs of life whatsoever, meaning this is a failure, a terrible, unsuccessful resuscitation. I wish to high heaven he'd had some veins to work with, as it's frustrating having a skill that could help and knowing I was unable to execute it effectively. *At least I didn't crash the ambulance,* I think.

The medical team is all gowned up and ready to receive us. There is a room full of nurses and at least three doctors and they're all at the ready for us to wheel inside.

'Hello, come on in, let's get a handover please,' the staff specialist says in a calm voice.

'Hi team, we will transfer him over then give you a handover,' Amanda says, as the medical team all stand back and let us manoeuvre the stretcher. With three sets of hands on either side of the board, the transfer is prepared.

'One, two, three, lift!' she calls out.

As one we lift the board over to the bed and carefully roll the toddler off. Chest compressions are recommenced immediately.

'Thanks. We have Toby, a thirteen-month-old boy who was found floating face down in a play pool forty-seven minutes ago. Mum commenced CPR no later than three minutes after he was immersed. He has been monitored in asystole throughout. There have been no signs of life throughout. We have given him 2.6 milligrams of adrenaline. He is intubated with a size four ET tube. He has not had a return of circulation as yet. Total down time is now fifty minutes.'

'Thanks, guys. Where are the parents?'

'They should be arriving now, the police brought them up.'

'Thank you. Send the parents in when they come, please.'

We reverse the stretcher out of the resuscitation bay and meet outside for a chat. We've completed the whole job in less than one hour. The trainee is nowhere to be seen, which concerns me a little. I saw her five minutes ago in tears behind the ambulance and wanted to see if she is okay. Now that I have the time to do that I glance around the parking bay, but she has probably ducked into the bathroom to tidy herself up. I know I will catch her soon.

'Thanks, everyone,' Amanda says.

We look at each other, pulling off gloves and straightening our hair. I take a big breath in and out.

'Are you okay?' I ask.

'Yeah, I'm fine. We probably stayed on scene too long but I wanted to secure that tube,' Amanda says.

'I totally agree. I think clinically we did okay but I completely stuffed the cannula, I'm so sorry. He had nothing!' I say. 'Pretty full on, though. God, the poor parents. You did great back there, mate. Are you okay?' I put my arm around Amanda's shoulders for a second as we walk back to our truck.

'Oh, I don't know about that,' Amanda says. 'I opted to put the drugs down the tube and in hindsight I'm not sure if that was the right thing to do.' She shakes her head a little and walks off to the bathroom.

We mooch around feeling pretty sad about the whole affair and go through the motions of cleaning up again. We strip the stretcher of the used linen and replace it with clean linen. It usually takes about twenty minutes to run through the cardiac arrest protocol and to pronounce a person dead, this timing usually coinciding with our clean-up being complete. Once we have finished the restocking of equipment and general cleaning, we would make our way back inside the emergency department to see where the team is up to. To my shock and surprise, when I stick my head into the resuscitation bay they're still working on the child.

My intention had been to pass on my deepest condolences to the parents, having assumed by now the little boy would have been pronounced dead. But what I see is a very different story: Dad is now in the room, and he is holding Mum. They're standing on the outer circle as the team of doctors and nurses continue working on the little boy.

'Come on, Toby! Come on, little mate, pull through!'

Oh my God. Intense!

Nobody tells the parents to get out or to be quiet. The staff specialist stands at the end of the bed directing his team.

Amazing, I think, surprised that they're still working almost ninety minutes later. It's as if the head specialist is conducting an orchestra. He lifts his hands and points calmly to the monitor and requests another drug be drawn up. Everyone with their clearly defined roles responds to his commands.

Then he crosses his arms and says: 'Okay, stop compressions. Let's see what's happening.'

To my absolute shock, there is a response. Little Toby has an output, his heart is generating a pulse!

'Come on, baby!' cries the father again. The emotion is intense, and it feels as though we are all urging the spirit back into his little body. For more than ninety minutes the team has worked on him; they're not going to give up.

'Come on, mate! We need you, mate! Don't die, little buddy,' Dad calls out again.

I think we all want to call out loud, that one voice airing our collective mind. The doctors and nurses calmly perform their actions. The parents are standing to the side but are very much a part of the process. They keep calling out to their child, begging him not to die. I am in awe of the fight for life, which stands in stark contrast to my hopeless state of mind that decided he was dead some time ago.

Duty calls us to the next case and we reluctantly leave the scene of the resuscitation. There is no immediate closure for us, no opportunity to express our support to the parents. With heavy hearts we move on to the next case of the day, unaware that little Toby is being wheeled upstairs to the intensive care unit with a heart that is beating.

'Nine-eighty-four, sorry to do this to you, but there is a motor vehicle accident down the road. I am going to have to ask that you clear.'

'Nine-eighty-four copy that.'

Before I step into the truck I find the trainee. 'Hey, Cheryl, you did great on that job,' I say. 'It's the worst job we do, but they're few and far between, you know. You handled yourself really well, okay?'

'Yeah, thanks, it was just really sad, sorry,' she says as she wipes a tear away.

'And it's okay that you're having a human response, too. Stay and talk to your partner, we've got another job.'

'Oh, I'm fine, really.' I'm not convinced, and also have tears in my eyes.

The next job is negligible, and the afternoon rolls on quickly as we do job after job. I feel sadness for most of the day at what I still believe is the premature end to a tiny life. Before I know it a whole week has passed, and the sadness begins to fade. When I get the phone call from Amanda I swear I nearly faint on the spot.

'Hey, Sandy, I just wanted to let you know I visited little Toby yesterday. He is doing just fine.'

'What?'

'Yeah, amazing, I know. I phoned the hospital to see what happened and they told me he maintained his output and they removed his ventilation support as he was breathing well on his own two days later. He's on the ward, mate. They reckon he doesn't have any brain damage, either.'

'You're kidding me, right?'

'Go and see for yourself,' she says. 'Apparently the mum wants to thank us all and the media unit is doing a bit of a thing about it.'

'Wow! Well, thanks for the call, and I'll see you soon, I guess.'

Then the tears come. My worst effort at cannulation yet and he's alive! A failed resuscitation in my mind, and he is alive! An hour and a half with no pulse of his own and he is alive! Cardiac arrest causing asystole, and he is alive! Every part of my hopeless mind thinking the worst and he is alive! All those statistics telling us he would never survive, that kids rarely survive near drowning, and he is alive!

There are so many things that seem miraculous about this incident. There are some scientific explanations thrown around in the discussions that follow, such as his core temperature being so low it contributed to his survival, and I completely accept this. However, I can't help but believe it's a miracle.

There is just no telling what will happen. Our very best efforts can still result in death, yet in this case our failings didn't seem to matter. Sometimes the power of love helps people depart and sometimes it helps them to stay but, really, who would know what's best for each soul? Sometimes all the love in the world and the very best treatment will not keep someone here.

On this occasion, perhaps love helped sway the outcome. There is a part of me that wants to believe love is so powerful but I really don't know. All I know is I'm completely shocked by Toby's survival and humbled at the same time. I was so sure he was gone, but what I learned is that I should never be so sure. It was the last time I ever felt so sure about someone either living or dying, the last time I questioned the power of hope and the last time I was so certain about an outcome.

Waiting at the ambulance station six weeks later, I feel strangely nervous. We are all exchanging pleasantries when I hear a voice calling out 'Ambyonce! Ambyonce!'

There is a pitter-patter of small feet and a mother's voice says: 'Toby! Here darling, let's see the paramedics then look at the ambulance.'

I turn around and see him running across the plant room floor.

Oh my God. There he is – the same little kid who lay lifelessly on the nature strip. The tiny arm I'd attempted to stick the cannula in was flapping about excitedly. He was of course completely oblivious to his near-death experience.

Everyone's face lights up with wide smiles and tears fill every eye. Toby happily extends his arms out for a hug and I am completely gob-smacked; I have no words for this moment. It's as though angels are singing, as though he was touched with a magic wand and simply came back to life.

Little Toby can't contain his child-like joy, running outside and yelling at the ambulance: 'Ambyonce!' His smiling face lights up the room and his effervescence is incredible.

'The doctors tell us he has some deficits but we can't tell. It's like it never happened. He is not even afraid of the water,' Toby's mother says.

She is holding Toby now and seems relaxed. We are all lucky enough to get a hug from him too. We spend the next hour having photos taken, inside the ambulance, outside the ambulance.

I am awestruck the entire time. Who says miracles don't happen? Every cell in my body is alive as I witness what can only be described as miraculous. I am in awe of the power of love and of life. Something released from me that day, some belief I was holding that it is my responsibility to bring people back to life. I can see now that it's not up to me, it is not within my control. It is my responsibility to do the very best I can, but whether someone lives or dies is out of my hands and very much in the hands of the universe.

This demonstration that life can return even in impossible circumstances reminds me that, really, I play a small part, because I am also aware that even in the event of 'perfect' circumstances people still die. I am left in awe at the great mystery of life and of love. Hope, a mighty force and one of love's languages, is a gift that is given to me this day.

3

IT COULD BE WORSE ...

I am going to smile like nothing's wrong, talk like everything is perfect, act like it's all a dream, and pretend it's not hurting me. – Anon

As we drive towards the accident, I cannot contain my anxiety. Fear is dripping into my stomach, saturating me and burning me like acid. My palms are sweating. I'm not driving today and it seems I'm working with Sydney's worst bloody driver! Have I overdosed on coffee? I feel shaky as hell. I wish I were driving; we'd be halfway there by now.

Get your shit together, mate! For God's sake, can you drive any slower? I think, as my partner struggles to get out of first gear. I don't think he knows where he's going, but I don't know him very well so I'm not comfortable asking him if he knows the address.

While he struggles to get the vehicle moving, I busy myself with my own tasks. I will need to get my helmet and reflective vest on. That's pretty straightforward, so I reach down to my helmet bag as we finally hit a decent speed. There is some confusion about what's happening at the scene of this emergency – the data terminal initially reported injured adults but now it's beeping furiously, alerting us to injured animals as well. Maybe they hit a dog, I think, as I try to focus and prepare myself for what lies ahead.

The siren is blasting, causing floods of anxiety to rip through my stomach. Because of my sweaty hands my fingers slip on the zipper of the helmet bag. I can't undo the bloody thing, and I know I only have minutes before I'll be looking into the eyes of the injured. If I don't get this helmet on my head I risk being in trouble not only from Work Cover but also the cops, let alone my supervisor, who will tear shreds off me for not being prepared.

I yank the zipper in frustration, trying to force it open, but it catches a thread and jams. I force it in the opposite direction and the thread gets caught deeper in the mechanism – I can see it tangled inside and every yank just makes it worse. My sweat coats the zipper like oil. I can't get the grip I need to yank it open, meaning I'll have to cut the bag. My trauma shears should do the job, so I rummage through my thigh pocket. Where the hell are they? I take my seatbelt off to give myself some more room to move: I'm so desperate to sort myself out, I decide to risk it. I need to spin around a bit, reach down to my thigh pocket and get my shears.

My partner is driving like a maniac. I don't know who this guy is, though he looks vaguely familiar. I get the sense we may have worked together years ago, but he has a beard now and I can't quite place him. Why is he driving like a maniac? *Slow the fuck down!* I think, as he sends us sideways on the last turn. My head strikes the window and it pisses me off. As my left temple hits the cold hard glass I'm startled: I feel confused, like I need to wake up, like I can't quite put these pieces together. Usually I can trust my partner, but I feel so out of control here, like my partner has gone mad and I don't know what to do.

This feeling of distrust makes me think it's not safe for me to say anything, so I swallow my resentment even though it sears my insides. It's like swallowing knives, and they slice me up. I can taste my own blood. *Get yourself together, woman! You are not bleeding!* I think, trying to coax myself into a normal state. We are moments from the scene, and I still don't have my helmet on.

Shit! I take to the helmet bag with my trauma shears, cutting straight through the zipper, desperate to get the bloody thing out. But my shears are blunt! I squeeze as hard as I can but the strength in my hands has gone. Usually the shears are good with thick material, but I can't seem to get the grip right. It seems to take forever, and the bag ends up in tatters; at least I get into it.

My heart sinks: the helmet isn't there. I can't believe I've left my helmet at home. *Who does that?* I think, cursing my own stupidity. *You idiot!* I'm terrified of the consequences and not sure what to do. The siren screams and I hate feeling like I'm in the limelight, that everyone can see me but I'm not ready, not even kitted out appropriately.

Usually I would say something. This is such a rare occurrence, not being able to lean on my partner, but I cannot rely on him, I don't trust him. I feel scared for my life right now. Nothing is going right and it's all moving so fast.

There is a very slim chance there's a spare helmet in the back of the ambulance, as we sometimes carry them for our student ride-along. We had a student in the back with us last week, but I can't remember if we were in this ambulance or another one. I think we were in car 424, and if I just stick my head out of the window for a second I'll be able to see the number on the side of this ambulance. Usually I would be happy to do this but today I'm scared my head will get smashed against a tree if I stick it out. The thought of my brain being smeared all over the place sends a wave of nausea through my guts. That coffee is about to come up, I'm sure. I stare straight ahead and take a deep breath. It's like breathing concentrated adrenaline, and my heart thunders in my chest and throat.

Like a crazed rally-car driver my partner launches us over the final hill, with us even becoming airborne for a second. He is intensely focused to the point of looking crazed, and as the wheels hit the road again I'm sure my own eyes are as black as his. My nerves feel fried. My hands are shaking and my mouth is dry.

The downhill section of road gives us a few seconds of perfect view, and I can see the carnage. Debris is spread for one hundred metres or more. *How fast were they driving?* I wonder, trying to do the math and work out the mechanism of the accident. It looks like a plane has fallen from the sky, there's so much twisted metal.

'What the hell?' I say, as my face freezes in shock.

The vehicles are on their side and smoke is billowing from a small hatchback. We are still fifty metres from the crash when my partner unexpectedly slams on the brakes. The staccato grind of the braking system is the only thing that prevents me flying through the windscreen and I press my hands into the dash to stop myself from face planting.

'Shit, mate! I don't have my seatbelt on, are you right?' I shout at him, mortified that the words even left my lips but furious that he slammed the brakes on so hard when he knew I was unrestrained.

'Get it together, Macken! Do you even know what you're doing?' he says, full of scorn.

Clearly he's not on my side, but he has a good point: I feel so out of my depth today. Even worse, I'll have to approach this tangled wreck with no helmet and no safety vest. It feels as though I've come to work with no clothes on.

There are three cars and one is still smoking. The smoke is thick, and I can't tell how many people are inside. Beyond the overturned car, the twisted metal of the other vehicles is strewn across the road. An engine block has somehow separated from one of the vehicles and is sitting in a pool of glistening green radiator fluid. Random items of clothing are scattered around and a teddy bear lies in the middle of the road, staring into space. Two of the vehicles have hit head on. One human body is cut in two, the torso lying motionless on the bonnet with the fingers still moving. This is not good, not good, not good.

I can use these few moments before I get to the first patient to calm myself; a few deep breaths usually ease my nerves. I slowly approach the side door of the ambulance to pick up the gear. Through the eerie silence comes the sound of the engine from one of the vehicles and the low, constant moaning of a woman. She is almost inaudible, but every so often I hear 'help me, please'.

My hand is shaking so violently I can hardly manage the task, but I must get this gear to her. A few more deep breaths and my focus shifts from the kit to the scene. My partner is nowhere to be seen. I can only assume he is giving a report over the radio, so I make my way towards the direction in which the voice calling for help had come.

My boots striking the roadway now is the only sound I hear. For some reason it reminds me of a teacher walking down a corridor at school when I was in trouble – I haven't done my homework and I've been found out. I'm a cheat, a fraud, and everyone knows it.

I listen intently for the woman. She was screaming and then after I could hear a low voice, but now she is silent. *Which one is she?* I know I have to leave the dead ones and get to the ones who are still alive, but they all look dead. There are two passengers behind the ejected body, however, I have a gut feeling the woman's voice was coming from the burning car so I go there first.

It's getting dark; it seems night has descended upon us quickly tonight. If I had my helmet, I would just turn on my headlamp. *Idiot!* I say to myself, cursing my very bones for forgetting my helmet.

The smoke is so thick, it is already giving me a headache and drying my throat.

'Please, help me.' I hear the words coming softly from within the burning vehicle. I place the equipment on the road and get as close to the side door as I can. The vehicle is on its side, so the woman is likely to be on the ground. I can either attempt to peer over the door and down in through the window that is facing the evening sky, or I can drop to the ground and attempt to make contact through the inch of space between the road and the smashed window.

The most logical choice is the ground, so I drop to my knees and move as close as possible to the window. The smoke is rising, giving me a brief respite from the fumes. For a moment I can't work out who's trapped – her or me? I shake my head, trying to clear it. Another deep breath, exhaling as much of this adrenaline as possible; it's messing with my thinking.

My knees feel warm and for a brief second it's soothing, then I look down and realise blood is pouring from the wreckage. There must be at least a litre here; I'm soaked in it.

'Help me, please, are you there? Hello? Is help here?' the woman says, desperately. *Oh my God!* I think. I have a bandage in my hand, and I know I can stop the bleeding. I just need to get to her.

'Please, my leg, I'm hurt, are you there? Is anybody there?' she says. She can't see me, the door is blocking me. If the fire brigade were here, this door would be cut off in two minutes. *Where the hell are the firies?* I think, frustrated. They're usually first on scene, where are they today?

'Yes! I am here, help is here, love. What's your name, dear?' I call

44

out. Blood is still seeping out through the smashed window. The car is tipped on the driver's side, and she is lying on the window against the road. The broken glass must have cut her. The blood is thick and red, which means it's arterial blood. As the woman's blood empties out her heart rate will increase, as it tries to maintain her blood pressure, and this will in turn increase the rate of blood loss. The only remedy is direct pressure on the wound to stop the blood flow.

'I'm here, help is here, can you see where you're bleeding, ma'am?' I ask. 'I need you to put direct pressure on it for me. I'm trying to work out how to get to you.' My words echo in the night air.

'Hello? Are you there? I am bleeding so much, can you help me?' she says again.

'Yes!' I say. 'I know you're bleeding, can you see where it's coming from?' I ask again. 'I need you to tell me what part of you is bleeding, love, we just need to put a bit of pressure on it. We will be with you as soon as we can get in,' I call out again, but my words are overwhelmed by the noise of the fire.

'I'm bleeding so much, are you there? Can you help me? It hurts. Hello?'

Fuck! I think, *where in God's name has my partner gone? If he were here, I could at least get a lift up and step in to the cabin. I know it's possible, but it's a two-person job. Where the hell is he?*

Frantically I search my mind for other solutions as the seconds turn into minutes and the minutes drain away. The distant, high-pitched scream of another siren alerts me that help is coming; it sounds like the fire brigade, thank God. What a sweet sound that is, another siren. At least I think it is a siren, as it fades somewhat. I second guess myself – could it have been a bird?

I swing my head around so wildly I hear my neck crack. *Oh no, you don't! Not today!* I think, as I freeze. With disc bulges in my spine from years of lifting and straining on the job I've become prone to acute neck spasms, and this is about the worst possible time for one. I can feel the muscles tightening, and shooting pain begins to radiate up the side of my neck and into my head.

Sometimes a shoulder massage can stop a full-blown muscle spasm, but this is not the time or place. However, if my neck goes I won't be able to help anyone! I get into a more upright position and massage my shoulder and neck a bit. I get some relief, but nowhere near as good as my massage therapist gives. *God, what I would do for a massage right now*, I think. The pain is becoming unbearable. I know this feeling – I will be immobile in a few minutes. It already feels like I've been hit with a taser between the shoulder blades.

Two more breaths, I think. *Just let the breaths release the muscle pain, it's only pain, you can move through this.* I pray for quick relief.

Another surge of rage floods through me, and I know this rage is contributing to the muscle spasm. My muscles are screaming. They're angry! I know intuitively that they're angry with my partner. *Where the fuck is he?* I turn my head slowly, scanning the surroundings. I need help here, and even though he's an arsehole surely he can still help!

How very wrong I am. In absolute shock and disgust, I see him – and he's on his goddamn phone! He's sitting in the driver's seat of the ambulance, texting! I cannot believe my eyes.

'Hello? Is anybody there?' The woman's voice again. It is barely a whisper now as the blood trickles metres away from the car, down into my socks. I'm lying in a pool of her blood, but the warmth is only momentary. I feel cold, which makes my jaw clench and my teeth chatter. The chattering is so violent I can't speak.

'Urggh, eeeer, urggg,' I say in response to the woman's calls for help. I want to scream, 'I'm here! I'm here! You're not alone!' but I can't say a single word.

'Please, anybody. Help me,' she says, groaning now.

'I'm here with you,' I say, but it comes out as a whisper too quiet for her to hear.

'Please,' she says, in a final whisper. 'There's no more time.'

Her blood empties onto the roadway. I hold the bandage in my hand, this useless bandage, so close but so far. She has no idea I'm here. She thinks she's alone and it breaks my heart. I hate my partner for this; if he weren't wasting time I would be inside the wreck with her.

My jaw is locked now, my throat completely dry. I am a barren desert of terror. It is as if the woman's terror seeped out of her body and I soaked it up, filling me. I'm dying here, too: we are all dying, and my idiot partner is texting, oblivious.

With one last attempt to clear my throat, which feels as though it has closed over, I scream. I scream with every ounce of my being. I channel every emotion I've ever had to help free my voice, to release this pain, to alert my partner that I need help. My mouth opens and I let it rip.

Silence.

My mute scream goes unnoticed. I want to punch a wall, but instead I slam my head hard on the ground. I knock myself out and my own blood begins to flow. I hear my skull crack, and it feels as though a gun has gone off in my head.

* * *

I sit bolt upright, drenched in sweat. *Where am I?* My heart's pounding, I'm breathing fast and I can't control it. My face and hands are numb and my fingers are locked in a claw grip so tight it hurts.

'Babe, are you okay?'

I know this voice, it is my boyfriend. *What the fuck is he doing at work?*

'Babe,' he says again. 'Are you okay?' I can hear him, but my mind returns to the back of the ambulance. Now I have to find him a helmet, too!

'Holy shit!' I say, as my breath heaves in my chest.

My boyfriend gets out of bed and turns on the light – and I see the familiar items of furniture, the wardrobe, my clothes on the floor and flowers by the window.

'Babe, I think you were having a bad dream,' he says, gently placing his hand on my shoulder.

'Yeah, right, shit,' I say. 'I need some water.'

He heads to the kitchen. The feelings are still with me, so fresh, so real, but they are fading as my breathing slows.

'Do you want to talk about it, sweetheart?' he asks tenderly. The dream's details are fading as I realise with relief that this night terror is not real. That woman trapped in the car is okay, a figment of my imagination. My failure is just a fear, and this dream is just a manifestation of my traumatised consciousness.

I drink the cool water, which moistens my dry throat, and I release my breath in a long sigh. The clock reads 03.20 – just two more hours to sleep before work.

'It's okay, babe, I just had a work dream,' I say, as I drop my shoulders and sigh again.

'Are you okay, sweetheart?' he asks again.

'I'm fine, babe, I'm fine,' I say, falling back onto the bed, cold from all the sweat. He holds my hand, which is no longer locked in spasm, and I soften a little. We lie there in silence for a few minutes. He knows not to push the point and is well aware of the trauma processing that comes up in the wee hours of the morning. His presence soothes me and the touch of his hand reminds me that although I carry this burden in the recesses of my mind, I am not alone. Love is here, through his presence and patience, and it soothes and holds me.

Eventually sleep returns and, with it, my nerves settle. I finally get some rest. When the alarm sounds at 5.30 am my memory of the dream has all but faded. The whistle of the kettle calls me out into the world once again and I bury my insecurities, pull on my uniform and prepare myself for the real world – ready to answer those calls for help.

Three times, no less, do I check my workbag to ensure there is a helmet inside. Of course there is, I have never been without it. It's funny how the insecurities that surface in the dreamscape can make their way into real life. But then again, who's to say those dreams are not real? My nervous system experiences all of it as real, despite the fact my mind manufactured the images and the story.

The patience and tolerance expressed by friends and partners in these times form the avenue for love's return. Sleep is not always restful for a paramedic, and fatigue becomes our constant companion. There is always great power in the simple gift of a glass of water or a hot cup of tea!

4

AMBO FAMILY LOVE

*From the ashes a fire shall be woken, A light from the shadows
shall spring; Renewed shall be blade that was broken, the crownless
again shall be king. – J.R.R. Tolkien*

There is a certain comfort that comes from being able to explain
in detail the various difficulties we as paramedics encounter on the
job. The conversations we have with each other, recounting the
challenges, triumphs and failings, are all part of a very important
process. Many of the incredibly intense scenarios occur without
witness in dynamic circumstances.

When we're called to an emergency there are so many variables,
and we learn so much from retelling our experiences with each other.
The stories we share help us learn, from each other's mistakes as
much as from our successes. We simply cannot prepare for many of
the scenes we enter.

Take, for example, the task of intubation – passing a long plastic
tube through the vocal cords to open and protect an airway. This
procedure is usually performed in operating theatres with the luxuries
of good lighting, a medical team and a patient who has not eaten for
at least a few hours. Mostly we are intubating adults who are in the

process of dying; rarely will it be a child. Of course, these children have not fasted, and tummies full of food or pool water make our job very challenging. Can you imagine our rising frustration with trying to intubate a child who has two minute noodles tangled around his vocal cords, preventing movement of air into or out of his lungs, after he has been pulled lifeless from a swimming pool? A task that should be quite simple is made impossibly difficult because of two minute noodles!

Semi-digested food breaks apart easily. If we can only get the noodles out air would go in, and yet they keep breaking apart on contact, making it nearly impossible to remove them completely. We lose precious seconds to two minute noodles – a failed resuscitation with noodle debris all through the airway gear. It's not our fault, of course, yet uncomfortable feelings remain, feelings that are reflected in these recurring questions: could we have done things differently? Could we have done more? The discomfort remains long after the clean-up is complete.

There is unspoken relief, gratitude and respect when paramedics laugh about the persistent, repugnant smell of burnt, wet human tissue that gets stuck in your nostrils days after you've attended a burns victim, regardless of whether or not you touched the patient. There is that moment of empathy when you take over the truck in the morning and the nightshift team say the night was 'shit'. We know what they mean in just that one syllable. Nothing more needs to be said, it's enough to make them a coffee so they can get home to bed in one piece. We've all been there, we all know what it's like.

When we describe ourselves as a 'family', it's because we see each other in our best and worst moments. I may not be my colleague's wife, but as his work partner I see him sweat as he tries in vain to resuscitate the child, the tears he tries to hide and the images from which he'll protect his wife. And he will see me hold the grandmother's hand as she passes, quietly saying a prayer to honour her when no family is there to do so. And unless you've actually seen a crazy cat lady breastfeeding her cats, you'll never appreciate how funny one glance from your partner can be: the one look that implies a serious concern for the cats! Then the conversation that later moves to 'lactation' issues in sixty-year-old women and the confusion: what drives a cat to suckle a human nipple? Can it happen without training?

These reflections, which so frequently stray into areas of great taboo, are the very experiences that bond us in a deep and secret way. We don't talk about the details often. Usually we are more concerned about where to find the next coffee but the bonds are there, they're real and strong. I have shed more tears from laughing with my colleagues about the hilarity of life than I have in crying over the horrors.

Obviously there are many tears we never shed – most of them, in fact. If I cried at every sad event I simply wouldn't be able to do my job. Yes, it is sad when tragedy occurs, but the truth is I sometimes have all of thirty minutes between jobs and the next patient deserves my attention and care too, so I need to move on swiftly. Natural human emotions get stuffed down somewhere inside us and it's not until tragedy hits my own world that I'm even aware of the deep emotional pain I have buried inside of me.

Being a naturally positive and resilient person, I tend to bounce into a good place on most days. Even in the post-nightshift haze of exhaustion and disorientation, a coffee gets me on track quickly. I have seen a lot of trauma, but who hasn't? Adopting a 'such is life' attitude keeps me in the realms of acceptance and this keeps me travelling along well.

This ability to swiftly move on after a traumatic event can leave us feeling falsely immune to life's tragedies. I'm strolling along in the sunshine on another glorious autumn day in Sydney when the phone rings. My long-term workmate never calls me, so when I see his name come up on the screen I wonder if perhaps I should be at work. I look at the time; it's midday, way too late to get that sort of call. I feel a vague reluctance to take the call but my curiosity gets the better of me, and I answer.

'Hi Sandy, it's Peter. Steven killed himself. I wanted to tell you before you heard on the grapevine,' he says, straight to the point. In typical ambo fashion he passes on the information clinically, not dressed up in any sentimental bullshit. Coming from this person, it lands soft enough. I appreciate he's taken the time to call me and I know he's been close friends with Steven for many years now, so this call was not an easy one for him.

'Shit,' I say. 'Serious? When? How?'

'They found him last night.'

'Right,' I say. 'Shit, that's pretty full on. Thanks for letting me know, I guess we will be in touch soon. Take care, hey?' I respond, and as the words leave my mouth I become numb and a bit lightheaded. I feel as though I might faint. I turn around immediately and walk back down the street, in the direction of a friend's place; I feel as though I'm about to vomit. Something is imminent but I'm not sure what it is. My feet walk down the street towards her house. I feel like an animal that is wounded and about to die, in desperate need of a safe place. My instincts are walking me, like the instincts that walk you to the toilet before you are aware you are about to lose the contents of your stomach.

He is one of our own and he is dead. It feels like a dam is about to burst open in my heart. The fact that he was once my boyfriend and I knew it would come to this one day makes the moment even more intense.

I walk in through the front door of my friend's place and I'm met with a face of loving concern; this is very out of character for me, to just turn up like this.

'What's wrong?' she says as soon as she sees me.

'Steve killed himself,' I say as I sit on her couch.

'Oh darling, I'm so sorry,' she says, her words full of love and compassion. Like a wrecking ball, the love she offers me shatters my walls. All of my defences come crashing down. I drop my face into my hands and a wail erupts from the depths of my being. I start purging grief. My tears and screams are so forceful that my stomach muscles ache and spasm. Brief moments of respite allow me to suck in big lungfuls of air between pounding waves of desolation. I can barely hold my body on the couch as it twists and turns through the waves of intense emotion.

I can hear my friend's quiet words of support. 'Oh darling, I am so sorry. That's it, sweetheart, let the pain come up, I'm here.'

I feel like I'm vomiting grief: it emerges from my body in great waves of uncontrollable emotion. It's as if every single suppressed tear has seen the light and bolts straight for it. Millions of tears desperate for their own release rush to the surface and I scream them out. I have no control and my body is not my own. It is like a seizure; just like a patient with epilepsy who cannot control their seizures I cannot control my grief, and it pours out of me like a tsunami.

As a paramedic I have a well-developed ability to appear unaffected in the face of horrific events. I can pause, breathe and respond with the right words in a very calm way. A plane could fall from the sky and I reckon I wouldn't flinch. I'd see it happen, pick up my phone and start making the necessary calls, then head in to the station and sign on for duty.

To be able to act in the face of intense trauma, I learned to dissociate from the feelings they induce. I used to think this dissociation was emotional mastery but I was wrong, of course. However, having that control over my emotions has certainly come in handy more than once during my career as an on-road paramedic.

Some say hearts don't break, they bend; but something broke deep inside me on that autumn day. All that 'mastery' melted in an instant and I sobbed a million tears. Of course, all paramedics have seen many, many deaths, but it's not about death. It's the tragic irony of a paramedic choosing death when he had been devoted to saving the life of so many others. He couldn't save himself.

Some may say that starting in the job at the age of twenty robbed me of my innocence. I disagree; it robbed me of some ignorance, perhaps. I like to think I've gained an incredibly positive attitude towards life as a result of this work. Street-wise a little before my time and a bit cynical on a bad day, but I've been granted a vision of life that few can appreciate and from which many would run.

Dealing with suicide after suicide among my colleagues has been a different matter, however. There is a wound that is difficult to heal when these people we share so much intensity with opt out. The first one was shocking, the second distressing, the third had been my boyfriend and felt as if it broke me, the fourth a friend and it pissed me off. The next was unexpected and the fact he was attended by a colleague who would become another statistic himself only eighteen months later was utterly devastating. Another sad irony is that he was found by yet another colleague, who will now also be haunted by that same final image.

And so the bittersweet relationship between paramedics forms. On one level you trust your partner with your life. God knows, we're aware of all their dirty secrets! But then you never know what dark thoughts they entertain – never really know if perhaps they will be the next one to make that final decision that will crush us all again. In the meantime we keep attending to the general public, knocking on doors, bringing them back from death, patching them up, sorting them out and mending their wounds. Letting them go and moving on.

Perhaps if we put enough people back together, save enough lives and relieve some more pain we will somehow mend our own hearts. Maybe we all just have one collective pain and we're hoping to recover our own losses through resuscitating our patients. Maybe a little piece of ourselves comes back to us each time we get a heart beating again. And maybe every time we cry from laughing about a breastfeeding cat lady, another fragment of our broken hearts flies back to us and gives us the fuel to keep going in this crazy, passionate, painful and glorious world of the paramedic.

What I do know from my wealth of experience dealing with suicide is this: emotions are energy moving, and it is normal and natural. When I allow myself space to grieve, cry or sob like I am hyperventilating, I feel better afterwards. Exhausted, but better. This is something I resisted for too long, thinking it to be a sign of not coping. Now I know that on the other side of a good cry is often great relief.

I believe that at our core we paramedics are essentially the same, as each other and as the rest of humanity. Even though we might operate within a role that demands objectivity and pragmatism we also have feelings. How we appreciate and process these feelings in the moment and also in the aftermath of intense experiences can have a huge effect on our well-being.

Talking about it helps too. It's okay to say you're pissed off, angry, let down, exhausted, sad. Finding a mate you trust and letting them know what's going on in your head can shed light on things and often alleviate a great pressure. If you ever entertain the thought that you want to self-harm or kill yourself, for goodness sake, tell someone. This brings light into an otherwise dark inner landscape. There is always help available, and there is always an easier, softer way.

Sometimes people have particularly rough patches and nine times out of ten these times pass, but if you are concerned for a colleague, call them and ask, 'Are you okay?' Mention your concern. Be there for each other, speak kindly about others when they're not there and always assume that you and everyone else always does the best job they possibly can do.

Suicide is a permanent solution to a temporary problem. There is always another option.

5

TOWN HALL BALL TEARER

It's a dangerous business, Frodo, going out your door. You step onto the road, and if you don't keep your feet, there's no knowing where you might be swept off to. – J.R.R. Tolkien

The job comes down the line as a laceration to the arm, so I'm wondering why the call taker dispatched the intensive care truck. I roll my eyes and make a conscious decision to go with the flow and just do the job. Generally the intensive care ambulance is held as a resource to use for the sickest casualties, and when there is a choice of two ambulances and we get the job my mind questions the decision. Of course, the underlying belief is that a simple laceration doesn't warrant the highest clinical resource and the other ambulance should take the job. We all hear the jobs going down over the radio and know where each other is, and most of us like playing 'controller' in our mind.

The truth is, there is usually more information coming from the person calling the job in and the dispatchers will respond with the closest ambulance resource. They do an incredible job, our call takers and dispatchers. Sometimes the information they receive is very limited, and frequently it is coming from people who are extremely stressed out and panicked. It could be as little as one or two minutes into a triple-zero call that we paramedics on the road are dispatched and moving towards the job. A laceration to the arm doesn't sound very life threatening, of course, but when you consider this information might be coming from a third-party caller, the injury could be anything from a paper cut to the full blown Texas chainsaw massacre.

One of the most helpful leaps in consciousness I have made has been changing the belief that the controllers are dictating these choices. Somewhere along the way I decided to affirm that I work for the divine, and so I surrender to the process a lot easier and with minimal internal retaliation. Holding this belief allows me to accept with a lot more ease the decisions people make that determine the extent to which I can help. I relax nowadays knowing that I am at every job I am meant to be at, that I am not at jobs not meant for me. There are bigger wheels turning in this life, and as I humble myself to this reality my inner 'controller' has taken a back seat. It's a much more enjoyable way to live.

As the eyes roll on this night, I am not quite there yet. I am still thinking I know best; I think we are going to a simple laceration and this doesn't sound very life threatening at all. Little do I know how very wrong I am. Little do I know the dispatcher has made a great call sending us, and little do I know that pretty soon I will be wishing we were never put on the call in first place and that I would be stretched to my greatest capacity.

You can't beat the system, Sand, just do the job, I mentally coach myself.

It's around 10 pm on a mid-week night and Sydney's George Street is a clear run all the way to the scene, Town Hall train station. We read the notes in our data terminal, which is blipping away furiously to let me know there is further information. Usually this is repeated information, but I read it out regardless to satisfy my partner's curiosity.

'It says it is a twenty-five year old, lacerations to the arm, queried amputation,' I read aloud.

We both raise our eyebrows. I reach for a spare pair of gloves to hide in the roll of my sock, bringing the grand total of gloves to be taken into the scene to seven.

'Oh well, there is a god. Sounds like this one could have something in it after all,' I say as we whistle through the streets of Sydney, lights ablaze.

'Now, the patient is all the way down the bottom platform. He could be on the tracks, I don't know, it doesn't say, so we will have to take all the gear, okay? Collars, spineboard, drug kit, Oxy-Viva resuscitator, first-aid kit and Lifepak.'

Tonight I'm working with a young woman who is fairly new to the job. We have back-up from a double crew of two other young women who are also fairly new. In this particular situation I'm the senior clinician, so decisions on how to run the job, how to treat the patient and how to organise the extrication are basically my responsibility. I am a new 'frog', or intensive care paramedic. Although I have years of experience in the city, I am new to this clinical role and to holding the responsibility of leading the scene. These are exciting times, and I am always happy to get good work.

Since I'm within the first two years of holding this clinical rank, every big job is adrenaline charged as it brings a unique set of tasks and challenges. I prepare myself mentally to make all critical decisions. I'm also mindful of the need to keep an eye on my colleagues and explain everything clearly. This makes it easier to work as a team.

We pull up outside Town Hall station less than six minutes after the triple-zero call has been received. We stack every piece of equipment known to humanity on top of our stretcher and make our way down to the platform in the elevator. We're met by a uniformed rail officer, who is pressing the lift button repeatedly as if he's typing in morse code: 'SOS … SOS'.

Strangely there is absolutely no one around; we seem to be approaching the ghost town train platform. We have to take the final level on the stairs, so with two heavy bags each we make our final march to the patient.

I see the thick, bright red trail of blood making its way lazily across the platform and spilling onto the tracks before I see the body. Instantly I go into intensive care mode: *significant blood loss, major trauma. Minimal time to spend on scene. Scoop and run to St Vincent's hospital. We can be outta here in twelve minutes. Let's go!*

There are no set rules in this game, but usually when a person is lying semi-conscious on a sure road to death, bystanders will do their best to help. Of course, there are exceptions to every rule, and one of the beautiful aspects of the job is the unpredictability of human nature. Curve balls: we love them, and we're about to be thrown a few here.

A large pillar obscures the patient, so I can't see what sort of injuries he has. He is about fifty metres away from us and we're walking quickly. A man steps out from behind the pillar and is almost running toward us. This is not unusual, as bystanders often love to let us know they've just completed a first-aid refresher course and would like to help.

Cool, maybe this bystander can help us with some of this gear; I'm dying here, I think, while maintaining my cool demeanour.

The man appears to be in his late teens or early twenties and is now running toward us. His forehead is glistening with sweat and his eyes are wide.

'You fucking *cunts*! You fucking killed my friend, you cunts!'

OK, maybe he won't carry the gear.

This guy is mad. I don't think he knows who we are.

'Mate, we're the ambos. Can you take us to your friend so we can help him?'

'You fucking arseholes! Do something, you useless fucking pricks! He's gonna die! ARRRGGGHHHHH!'

He screams like a wounded bull, and I suspect he's in some sort of psychosis or has been using the crazy-making drug ice. In any case the anger and aggression is off the dial, so I immediately lean into the microphone of my portable radio and voice the duress code: 'car nine-eight-four, CODE ONE!', *send in the cavalry, baby!*

If the radio room heard my two-word request, we should have help very soon. Everyone in the area will be wondering what on earth is going on and if we are okay.

We're stopped in our tracks by this crazy man, who is the one actually killing his friend with every second he keeps us from him. But he's out of his mind, oblivious to the harm he's causing.

I cannot reason with him; my words don't reach him. I place all the gear on the ground and stand still. I remove a tourniquet from the first-aid box and hold it in my right hand.

The enraged guy is standing in front of the patient, who I now have in full view. He is clearly bleeding out and is covered in oily grease, which tells me he has been on the tracks at some point. His left arm has been ripped from the shoulder, with nothing left from below the elbow. His right lower leg is also missing. He is lying in a massive pool of blood, sort of squirming around in it. For a moment I think he looks like me when I sleep between night shifts in the summer: restless, and doing crocodile death rolls in the sheets.

'Youse fucking cunts have blood on ya hands now! My mate is nearly dead cause a youse. We weren't doin' nothing and ya fuckin' gone and done this, ya fuckin dog cunts!'

There are plenty of alarm bells going off in my mind at this stage and I think we should probably retreat. I stand still as the guy blows off more steam in my face. I glance sideways at the dark pool of blood. There is no more squirming and I suspect our patient is losing consciousness, but I can't turn my back on the madman. I need to pacify him. My ambo Terminator-style brain rapidly scans the situation in an attempt to come up with the best method to calm this guy down. It's still just me and my partner standing behind me; no cops yet. This lasts forty-five seconds but seems like an hour.

In my right hand I hold a tourniquet bandage, clutching the tightly wrapped length of rubber as if it were kryptonite. I'm holding it at shoulder height in full view of this man as if it were the absolute saving grace. My face is as expressionless as I can maintain. God knows, I don't want to antagonise him. He would have no idea how hard my heart is thumping right now, or that my hands are sweaty and my nervous system is so heightened I'm already considering how to calm myself prior to cannulating our patient.

'Your friend is going to die if I don't stop that bleeding,' I say to the man calmly but sternly. 'Do you understand me? And I am not moving until you step aside.' I am running completely on my intuition; time seems to slow down and every word matters. This guy is much larger than both me and my partner, and if he really wanted to hurt us he could. He could outrun us, tackle us to the ground and kill us. The split-second decision I have made to freeze and talk to him like this is as much about self-preservation as it is about helping the patient on the platform. Every case is different, and in a perfect world we would be nowhere near this degree of violent threat. Yet here we are, and it is critical that I somehow disarm him.

It's a stand-off. He is the biggest problem on this platform right now and our lives may also be in danger if he is not subdued.

'Fucking do something, you stupid bitch!' he yells to my face.

'Please move aside so I can help your friend. Nothing happens till you move right away, all the way over there. It's up to you now. He needs our help and you need to move away.'

By some stroke of good fortune my tourniquet manoeuvre works and the man storms off to the other end of the platform just as the boys in blue come running our way. I indicate to them with a single point of the finger.

'That guy!' is all I need to say to these angels in blue, our brothers and sisters in the police force. They can tell I'm pissed off, have heightened feelings and have been under threat. They busy themselves with Mr Angry.

Finally, after the longest two minutes I've ever endured, we gain access to our bleeding patient. Just as I suspected, his injuries are severe and his colour is bad. I can estimate his blood pressure by looking at him: sweaty and white at that age and with those injuries mean that his blood pressure will hardly generate a pulse. When most of the blood volume is on the outside of your body, you tend to look like this guy. When a person's blood pressure gets low enough, they go into cardiac arrest and die. One of the things we do to stop that happening is pump fluids into the vein and replace the volume with salty sterile water, which can give someone the chance to stay alive until a medical team replaces their blood loss with actual blood products.

I know we need to work fast to secure intravenous access and pump fluids back into his system. Unfortunately, it appears our patient has been drinking from the same fountain as the angry guy and is highly unco-operative. I am well aware he could simply be suffering the effects of shock, but judging by the way he's trying to rip his own flesh off near his amputated arm tells me there are probably drugs or alcohol in his system.

So here we are, four ambo women, gathered around a wriggling, near-death patient. We can hear a melee of some kind going on behind us involving increasing numbers of cops, railway staff and goodness knows who else. I'm aware that I gave myself a twelve-minute timeframe in which to be out of here and I have already blown this out by double. A seemingly simple scoop-and-run situation is being foiled because this guy is so heavily affected by drugs he is more interested in picking at his brand new stump than he is in letting us help him.

It can be tricky in these situations to try and figure out what has happened immediately prior to our arrival. As well as treating the patient and handling bystanders, we are also attempting to gather information about the events that caused the injuries. This information can be vital, as it lets us know about potential internal or head injuries or hazards. On this particular occasion it is very difficult to gather information because the only witness is now behaving in a rather psychotic manner, and the patient is very unwell and almost unconscious.

It is not until the police arrive and investigate the CCTV footage that we find out these two apparently drug-affected men were running around the underground subway. They were chased by some security staff and, in an attempt to avoid getting caught, hid down on the tracks behind a train that was stationary. When the train pulled out from the station, it knocked one of the guys to the ground and took off his arm and his leg, both of which are nowhere to be seen. It remains a mystery to us how he managed to find himself lying up on the platform; nevertheless I am happy about this, as it is much easier to treat him here than underneath a train. It is an almighty mess, but at least everything is visible.

I could really do with a towel at this stage. My boots are slipping in the pool of blood and I need the drug kit close by. My colleagues are tentatively trying to hold the patient down, and now 'Cranky Pants Sandy' joins the party. Maybe it was the abuse I copped a few minutes ago; maybe it is the fact that nothing is going smoothly here; or maybe it's the coffee entering my system. I don't know, but now I really have the shits.

'Guys, hold him down. I mean it. Get your hands on his collar and *hold him down!*'

I put the largest cannula into the vein in the crook of the patient's good elbow. Bingo! It's great when you get them in when it counts. I take one hand off his arm to grab some tape from next to my knee. In a nanosecond, he wriggles free of my colleagues' grip and rips out the cannula. *Oh shit!* I curse inwardly, wishing I could just scream at him to stop moving.

Whatever blood he has left in his system is now streaming out all over my leg. A lovely fresh pool of dark red blood is joining the giant frisbee-sized clot at the end of the platform. My team is sweating here, as we find ourselves in a situation that is as physically demanding as it is mentally. Things are not running smoothly; we are all well aware that we have an aggressive male a short distance from us and our patient is very uncooperative. 'Okay, hold him down now. I don't care if you have to sit on him. We have one vein left, okay? It's in his bicep. *Do not let him move!*'

My second attempt is also good. There is so much blood on the patient I'm cursing myself for not bringing a towel down with us. Nothing sticks on blood. Securing the line is like folding a paper plane under water, but there is one type of tape that does the trick every time: Coban, the paramedic's best friend. I know it's in that kit. God, I need that brown and stretchy Coban tape. You could tape something up under water if you need to, as it sticks to itself in a magical, mystical way.

'Mate, open up that kit there and pass me the Coban, can you?'

'The what?'

You're kidding me, aren't you?

'The Coban, mate. It's tape, brown tape. I need the tape to tie this line in. It's too slippery otherwise. Nothing is sticking. Try the left side there.'

My junior colleague starts digging around in the wrong box. I feel frustrated that things are so slippery and out of control, and it would be so easy for me to lose my cool and bark orders. I really want to get everyone on the team working well, so I refrain from barking at them and adopt an even calmer tone.

'That's okay, mate. I'll hold it in. Just draw me up some midazolam. We are going to have to sedate him.' The frustration and adrenaline seem to turn into fluid and pour out of me in the form of sweat. My shirt feels wet and my forehead is glistening.

The patient is still squirming around and is totally unmanageable, so I really have no other choice. Treating him is next to impossible as it's still taking four of us to hold him down.

'What does midazolam look like? Oh God, can someone show me how to draw it up? I'm not confident with this one,' the junior colleague says.

We've all been there. Not every ambo has the same skill set, and when something is asked of you and you don't know exactly what they are talking about because you're not at that clinical level it can be incredibly stressful. We all want to be slick and confident, but it takes years to get there. It also takes practice working as a team and managing different tasks. As much as I empathise here, the pressure has me sitting in a laser beam focus on what the patient needs. I need to get this medication prepared so I can manage the severe agitation of this very unwell patient. I know what needs to get done, but it feels as though we are being met with obstructions and blocks the whole way. Murphy's law states that everything that can go wrong will go wrong, and tonight I feel like living proof of this law. Nobody is at fault; it is just circumstances piled on top of us and we simply have to find a way through.

There is a part of me that wants to stand up and tell everyone I'm going home now. I just want to be at home under my doona watching *The Sound of Music*! You guys cool to handle the rest of this fiasco? Good, cos I am outta here. Keep ya Coban and do what you want with the job. See you tomorrow!

But, no, what really needs to come out in moments like these is a lot of patience, a calm demeanour; plenty of 'pleases' and 'it's okays', as nobody shines when they're shitting themselves. It's part of my job to support the staff and encourage them as much as possible, and it's amazing what emotions you can hide at these times.

'It's that little ampule there, love, just take it out for me and take over from holding the line in. I'll draw it up,' I say in the most loving and calm voice I can muster.

My colleague comes over to support the cannula in place so maybe there is a chance we can get this job back under control.

'We cannot lose this line, okay? Don't be scared to hurt him. Just don't let him move.'

I lean over to the drug box and slip over in a giant clot. Oh good, we're going from bad to worse. Right on cue!

I draw up the drug in an instant, then skate back over to the patient through the blood and breathe a sigh of relief when I see we still have IV access. I sedate him, and his muscles relax immediately. The junior ambos tentatively take their hands off him at my request.

For the first time in fifteen minutes we have control of this scene and the patient. A lonely bead of sweat rolls down my temple, attempting to sooth me. Futile!

I look up to see that our ambulance inspector has arrived. It's as though he has entered the scene through a plume of smoke, and I hear a chorus of angels singing as he walks calmly to my side.

'What do you need, Sandy?' he asks, adopting his own utterly perfected calm voice.

'Oh Stan, hi!' The faintest smile lifts my cheeks.

'Coban, Just Coban-tape, Stan. That's all I need.'

'Okay. Where's the Coban?' Stan replies simply.

He opens the kit and finds the tape straight away. He passes me the tape, and I secure the line just how I like to. Nothing is going to remove this line.

Stan has more experience in the job than I do in life. I know he knows just what sort of horror show took place here. It feels like the drama has long since subsided, even though we have only been on scene for a grand total of twenty-five minutes.

I don't need to explain anything; Stan has been there and done that.

'Do you need anything else, Sandy?'

'No, we are right to get moving now, Stan, thanks.'

He's on the phone to the hospital before we're in the truck and things are back on track, with the patient responding well to our treatment. In less than thirty minutes the whole job is over. We've driven the patient to the emergency department, unconscious but alive. The incredible staff at St Vincent's Hospital receive him well and have him straight off to the operating theatre. With the patient off the stretcher, we meander in momentary silence out to the vehicles to begin the clean-up.

It is not until I am halfway through one of the worst instant coffees I've ever had that I hear what happened on the platform behind the pillar. The rest of the team is talking excitedly about the capsicum spray that was raining down. One police officer is sporting a black eye from a punch in the face and several arrests were made.

It turns out my soothing manoeuvres didn't keep Mr Angry pacified for long.

In the aftermath of such mayhem I ponder the disappointing fact that next to no one knows the degree of difficulty that went into packaging that patient and getting him to hospital in a timely fashion. This, like so many other jobs we simply call 'good' work, will forever be unwitnessed, unseen and unrecognised. These are the images that flood my mind when asked innumerable times if 'they let you drive that big truck'. It is these memories and images of a difficult job done well by an all-woman double team that I recall when people seem shocked to know they 'let women work together' these days.

'Oh, if only you knew,' I think to myself with these questions.

It is not easy to advocate for the sick and injured when your life is being threatened. To think that I held up a tourniquet in the face of a psychotic, volatile man as if it were some kind of weapon in an attempt to bring reason to the scene shows the degree of vulnerability we experience on the front line of pre-hospital emergency care.

Thankfully I can rely on my peers at work , both the women and the men, to get it when I simply say that we just did a 'ball tearer'. I don't need a set of balls to know how intense that would be, nor do I need a set of balls to do the same work and face the same violence as any man in our profession – a fact that has been both liberating and terrifying at the same time.

6

LETTING GO

I am no longer the wave of consciousness thinking itself separated from the sea of cosmic consciousness. I am the ocean of spirit that has become the wave of human life. – Paramahansa Yogananda

The most precious and profound moments are usually unexpected. As we receive the call on this bitterly cold night to attend the old chap in Vaucluse, I'm certainly not expecting one. I am the treating paramedic officer so I sit in the passenger side of the ambulance as my partner looks up the address and drives out of the plant room and onto the back streets of Bondi. Once again, the pretty mix of red and blue light bounces off the street signs as we make our way silently yet swiftly through the streets toward our patient. It is a typical night shift at a local ambulance station: no specific expectations, but always being aware that anything could happen and something significant probably will.

'Oh yes, I know this address,' I say. 'I remember attending this guy a few weeks ago. Massive house, home nursing, super-stressed wife. I thought I was working with you, or was it Brendan?' I pop a piece of gum into my mouth.

'Must've been Brendan, I don't remember this neck of the woods,' my partner responds casually as we whistle through the streets.

'The wife was a little bit difficult last time, a tad controlling even,' I say. 'He's a quadriplegic and she cares for him at home. They're obviously well off as the house is amazing. We had to carry him down a couple of flights of stairs last time but it's okay, there's not much of him, he probably weighs only fifty kilos. Last time I got the impression that she wanted him alive for her own sake, you know? Doing everything possible to keep him alive. I just saw such suffering.'

It's interesting how I can pull a mental file of a job from the back recesses of my brain. All sorts of images and impressions come to me as I recall attending this address a few weeks ago.

I know he's very sick. He was gravely ill last time I attended; hardly 'quality of life', I recall thinking as we carted him off to hospital for a chest infection. The couple's home care is excellent, however: a full-time nurse and the latest in fancy hospital bedding. I know they're only going to call for the ambulance when it's really time to go to hospital. This lovely patient had some serious complications last time, and I suspect tonight will be the same if not worse. All these musings are how my brain prepares me to deal with the job. I excuse the occasional intrusive thought about Vegemite toast, promising myself a midnight snack after this job.

We pull into the street and once again we're graced with pop-star parking – right out the front of the house. We both alight from the vehicle, moving promptly but not rushing. You'll rarely see a paramedic rush; it is so much easier for us to think and attend to people when we're calm.

My partner and I don't need words, as we've both been around long enough to know what to do without planning it. I take the oxygen and drug kits out of the side section of the ambulance and stride ahead.

My partner takes the Lifepak from its resting place, the side door of the ambulance, and slides the door shut. The Lifepak weighs about ten kilograms and is bulky to carry, but it goes everywhere we go. To the untrained eye it might look like a television screen, especially when we turn it on and gaze at the squiggly lines. The Lifepak reads electrical activity in the heart and interprets these electrical impulses; then, with input from us, it delivers an electric shock to the patient that sometimes results in the return of a normal heart beat.

You've seen it on TV: an unconscious patient on the ground or a gurney, conductive pads connected to their chest and a paramedic calling out 'Everybody clear!' With the press of a button on the Lifepak, electricity passes along the wires and through the body, which often jolts dramatically in response. If we can get this shock delivered quickly enough, the heart in some cases will restart and the patient may survive. It is well worth its ten kilos.

As we approach the house a sensor picks up my movement across the beautifully manicured front garden, then lights switch on automatically and welcome us in. The house is huge. I wipe my boots on the mat more as a sign of respect than anything; the polished marble floor is no place for this filthy old footwear, but I'm guessing nobody will care.

I silently curse the grand spiral staircase as I lug the Lifepak up. I'm greeted with soft lighting, luxurious bone-coloured carpet and five or so very scared faces. They gesture me into a large bedroom, where a man lies in a hospital bed and a woman stands by his side. I take one look and I know he's close to death; he won't survive the night.

With dozens of concerns springing to mind, I immediately assess the most important factor. Is she ready? Is she ready to let him go? The man has wasted away to the size of a child, and I can see his ribs moving up and down. His laboured breathing has slowed. The room is like a toasty incubator protecting him from the world beyond the four walls, but nothing will pink up those blue lips or halt those twinkling little beads of sweat tonight.

It's an uncomfortable and difficult moment and I need to ascertain whether treatment will be purely palliative. His breaths are almost agonal – laboured and gasping. The agonal respirations of the dying can sound peculiar when we are so used to the way healthy people breathe on this earthly plane. Suddenly we have a person who is breathing like a fish out of water, staring into mid space and with his mouth moving ever so slowly open then closed. Not quite closed, though, just closed enough to allow for another effort to open and with great effort to draw in a little more air, but it seems ineffective, as if something is missing. It appears as though the life force is lacking in the air this body breathes.

I remember as a child going fishing with my father. We would be overjoyed to land a fish and watch it bounce around on the deck of our little wooden boat. The excitement would turn to curiosity, then urgency to return the fish to water as I watched it gasping. The fish would be opening and closing its mouth, starving for oxygen that the air simply cannot supply, certain death awaiting, until we removed the hook and returned it to the water.

Looking at this man, I see something similar happening. Just like the fish, this man needs to return to his ocean. We need to liberate him from his hooks and let him swim free. When we returned our fish to the water and I watched it swim away and disappear from sight, I understood it lived on, unhooked and free. This, I believe, is what happens in death: although a loved one disappears from our sight as their spirit escapes their physical body, they return to the infinite sea of consciousness and swim on, unbound and free.

The family members recognise me straight away, and while we exchange pleasantries I approach our patient directly and whip out a high-flow oxygen mask and slip it over his head. His eyes are half closed and I note the deep gurgling sound resonating in his chest.

'May I have a word with you in private, Sarah?' I say to the patient's wife, who is by his side.

She knows it; I know it. This is the end of the worldly journey for this man. *Oh, please God, help this lady let go, I cannot run this cardiac arrest*, I pray, as I lead Sarah out into a hallway out of earshot of her husband. We stand in what appears to be a giant walk-in wardrobe for a quick 'time out' chat as my partner begins to treat the patient. This pause in teamwork treatment of a patient is unusual but absolutely essential when death is expected, because the next of kin play such an important role.

'Sarah, your husband is very sick,' I say. 'He is a lot worse than last time. I need to ask you what you want us to do if his heart gives out tonight. Do you want us to resuscitate?'

It's always a gamble, offering the family power of choice. If they're extremely distressed and haven't accepted the imminent death of their beloved, they often request that we resuscitate. Frantic family members feel they can prevent death by requesting resuscitation, that we can somehow bring people back from the inevitable by pushing valiantly on their frail chests. People tend to feel a huge responsibility to keep people here, believing alive is always better than dead no matter how sick the person may be or how much they're suffering. Family members can feel guilty, unloving or unkind if they simply allow the dying process; they see pushing for resuscitation as an act of love.

There are of course plenty of situations that are reversible and effective CPR can save lives, but when a person is clearly at the end of their life, CPR means crushing ribs and preventing a dignified, peaceful passing. Paramedics are well trained in this area, and know the difference. Medical advice will always be to commence CPR if necessary, but once paramedics are with the patient many more considerations come into play.

If, however, the family accepts the imminence of death in a patient such as this, who has had a protracted, long-term battle with an incurable condition, then palliative and supportive care is an option that paramedics can offer.

'Resuscitation? No, no – he wouldn't want that,' Sarah replies, looking at me intently with distress in her eyes. Her look changes to horror as she clamps a hand over her mouth. 'Oh my God, can I even say that?' she asks under her breath. Tears begin to stream down her face.

I look into her eyes and place a reassuring hand on her upper arm, hoping to infuse her with courage and give her the message that she is not alone in this moment.

'Sarah, it doesn't mean we're going to withhold treatment,' I say. 'We will keep him on oxygen. We will keep him comfortable. I will pop a cannula in his vein so we can give medication, as he needs it. And, yes, it is okay to express to me whether he would want to be aggressively resuscitated or not given his current condition. We are going to continue to treat him supportively as we make our way to hospital. You're doing great, Sarah.'

Imminent death, much like imminent birth, can be incredibly stressful for those who are witness to it. In our culture it is not something that typically takes place at home, and it is rarely seen.

It seems strange to me that something we all must face is treated as taboo and met with such resistance, yet I completely appreciate the fear that arises when suddenly it comes time to say goodbye. Had I not experienced so many of these situations where the clinical decisions become automatic, perhaps I would also be overwhelmed. But here, tonight, I have more than a few years' experience as a paramedic and have witnessed many people deteriorate, and I can foresee the process. Being confident with the clinical process allows me to be present to the family's emotional process, which is a major priority this evening.

Families can go either way at times such as these: either fear will dominate and a thousand walls will spring up, or acceptance and love will dominate and we will bear witness to an intensely intimate and sacred moment.

When I first attended this patient a few weeks back it was fear, fear and more fear. It was barking orders and control; it was rigidity and harsh tones. Obviously I forgive all this as I acknowledge the anguish of nursing a much-loved partner who is dying.

Sarah is a different person tonight; perhaps it is now too painful for her to see her husband suffer. Who could know? She seems prepared for this moment. We move back into the bedroom, which looks more like a hospital ward: beautiful artworks decorate the walls and the carpet is soft to kneel on. Sarah climbs up onto the bed and nestles in. She cradles her husband's head against her breast and lovingly wipes the beads of sweat off his face.

The home-care nurse is busying herself with cleaning up as our patient has lost bowel control, another indicator he is on the way out. I look at my partner and indicate we'll need the stretcher set up downstairs. He disappears to get the equipment.

Mother nature takes control of death, just as she does of birth. The two are similar in that there is awareness that this is it, it's time, there is no stopping it. Anxious family members are in the house supporting from a distance but basically terrified. Paramedics are trying to think of the right words and often fumble their way through. The magic moments are often fleeting, especially when like tonight there is an extrication to consider and a patient who is still alive and in need of a little more care. Often it's only with hindsight that I can think *wow*, that was the night he passed away and we were all there together. It is very difficult for most people to be fully present amid such intense conditions and decisions.

The bed, which is quite low, has all the bells and whistles with a very complicated remote control that I can't work out for the life of me! I'm scared I'll eject the patient from the bed if I touch a button, so I kneel on the plush carpet to be at a more appropriate height. We've got a few minutes before my partner returns with the stretcher, and there is little more to be done treatment wise.

Our patient is drowsy. His eyelids appear too heavy for him to hold open and they slowly begin to close. He seems relieved to feel the closeness of his beloved. I think again of the moment Dad released the fish overboard, how it swam free and far out of sight. Our patient closes his eyes and I imagine his spirit starting to orient towards that same freedom. Sarah talks to him as she wipes the beads of sweat that continue to spring from his brow.

'Remember Hawaii, darling?' she whispers into his ear. 'Oh, it was so beautiful there. We loved it so much. Walking along the beach at night …'

Love is pouring out from this courageous lady. She looks at me and tells me they spent their honeymoon in Hawaii. 'It was David's favourite trip ever,' she says. The tears are falling down her cheek, but her voice is strong and her mind focused. David closes his eyes and she keeps talking. I am kneeling opposite Sarah on the other side of the bed and holding David's hand. For a fleeting second I wonder if he can feel it, whether it was fruitless because, after all, the man is a quadriplegic. Nevertheless, it seems right.

We are sharing one of those unexpected moments, fleeting yet divine. For a few brief seconds we have realised that nothing matters but love. When all else is gone, when we are at the end, stripped of everything, including our health, all that remains is love. As I kneel I bear witness to this love as Sarah holds space for her beloved and I hold space for her. The connection between these two is palpable. The last thing to hold on to is the unchangeable, indestructible connection of love. This love, which expands with their willingness to let go, is very beautiful, patient, soft and kind.

It can be difficult to sit still and silent and allow these moments although it is vitally important, yet my paramedic's instinct urges me to get the hell outta here! David needs an urgent transport; that jugular vein is good for a line; Vinnie's will have to know we're coming; we'll probably need an urgent assist load; how long is that pacemaker going to keep him alive?

Despite that I find myself kneeling by the bedside of a man who is passing away, cradled in the arms of his beloved who is truly a pillar of strength for him right now. I'm not tearing open little plastic packages to get to the next drug, not frantically popping lids off medications or preparing to start cardiac compressions, which is what I would normally do in the face of a pending cardiac arrest.

Instead I'm part of this magical moment, allowing, supporting, facilitating. I know Sarah is scared and I know David's spirit is ready to go home. He is worn out, ready to drop his body. I sense for a moment that the force of love is far stronger than the force of fear. I imagine fear has kept him here in his tired, emaciated body. He has held on until the very end, squeezing every possible last pump out of his heart, and now it is love that releases him. Somehow Sarah knows this, somehow she knows what she has to do; her own heart is guiding her.

As Sarah speaks softly to David about the times they've shared, he closes his eyes as if falling asleep. Her words settle him down and send him off.

His brow is covered in sparkling beads of sweat. Usually this would prompt me to work faster, treat aggressively, give more fluids, maybe some adrenaline – but not tonight. Tonight I am the support from which Sarah can draw strength. I am the attentive witness. I am the eye contact when she draws a breath between sentences. I am the smile and the nod that says to her 'you're doing great, you're not alone, everything is going to be okay'.

I am witnessing a deeply moving moment and mentally holding Sarah's hand as she does the seemingly impossible: she lets her beloved go.

Relieved by the family's consent to palliative treatment only, we go about the business of carrying David down the stairs and loading him into the ambulance parked out the front. It takes four family members to help us carry him on our sling-like carry sheet down the stairs. They're young and fit and I assume they're his sons. For the first time I make note of how many people are here; they must have been in another room. There are eight people walking with us as we push the stretcher down the driveway. It's cold and David is wearing black gloves and a matching black woollen beanie. Despite the chill in the air he is still sweating profusely.

It's so quiet in this suburban street. I lower my voice as we line the stretcher up then slide it into that back of the ambulance. There are two young men on either side of the stretcher holding David's hands. They try to push the stretcher into the ambulance. Their attempt to be helpful is obstructive and a little annoying, but I can see the benefit of allowing them to feel like they're contributing so I patiently let them get in the way. I know this night will be seared into their memories forever, that it is as much about them as it is about their father.

'Just mind yourself there,' I say. 'You'll have to let go of his hand so we can push the stretcher in.' The front wheels are on the runners and the stretcher is half inside the truck. The second phase of pushing the stretcher in requires two people, so I move to the back of the stretcher to help my partner. The family moves in to say goodbye.

'Bye Dad, love you, mate,' says the eldest of the boys. He kisses a patch of skin on David's head that lays exposed to the night air.

'See you at the other end, Dad,' says the younger of the sons. He leans in and tenderly adjusts his father's lopsided beanie. He holds his father's face in his hands for a moment and blinks away the tears.

Mindful not to rush anyone, I smile encouragingly as they each step up one at a time to say goodbye. Before shutting the doors, I invite Sarah to travel with me in the back. The last few precious moments are all hers. She touches David's face and speaks softly to him. The tears are gone for now and our ride is smooth.

Within half an hour we've handed David over to the hospital staff. Sarah has not left his side for more than a moment, and when I pass the family members in the corridor I direct them to the private room where they'll find David and Sarah. The two sons extend their hand to me and we exchange a firm shake.

'Thanks for bringing him in, really appreciate it,' says the younger of the two. I can tell he feels better now that they're in the hospital.

'You're most welcome,' I reply with a warm smile. The brothers' strides match each other as they slip in behind the curtain together to be with their dad. I wander out to the truck to find my partner ready to drive us back to the station for a cup of tea and Vegemite toast. It's past midnight now, after all.

Several hours later I hear that David passed away in that hospital bed with his family around him, not long after his arrival at the hospital. What a relief. Who could ask for more than to pass away surrounded by those who love you? I have a sense that all is right in the world. Just like the fish that has been freed from the hook and returned to the sea, the spirit swims free. The moment Sarah released the hook, David swam free.

This job could have run very differently if Sarah hadn't been ready to let David go. Her courage in letting go was such a critical factor. She held the key that unlocked the door to let all that love in. Although it was also love that spurred her previous fight to keep him alive, there is a perfection in it all.

Letting go is a process that occurs at various levels: mental, emotional, energetic and spiritual. We can mentally appreciate that a person is suffering but be unwilling to allow them to die because the energetic connection is so strong, and there is a part of us that would experience their loss as a death in ourselves. We may think someone is dead and gone only to find their spirit is our companion, still influencing our thoughts and decisions years after they have died.

It is fear that creates attachment, our failure to perceive that love and life can exist beyond the physical form we know. When we free ourselves of our attachments we are in with a chance to have love open its floodgates to us. Attachments to people, ideas, expectations and the past are like hooks holding us back; although it is usually a challenging and sometimes lengthy process, letting go brings freedom. In more recent times I have come to understand that by letting go of my attachment to the physical form of a beloved, that love is eternal and lives on even beyond the death of the body.

7

I'D GIVE MY RIGHT ARM ...

*Recognising our own mistakes helps us to empathise non-judgmentally
with others and helps us to understand their issues.* – Jay Woodman

The intercom calls me out of my deep sleep by repeating those god-awful numbers: 'Nine-eighty-four, nine-eighty-four on the air for a casualty thanks, nine-eighty-four.'

Faaaark off, my mind yells in protest.

There was a time when it didn't hurt so much but these days, ten years on, the 3 am wake-up call really hurts. As the adrenaline squeezes what little enthusiasm I have for the waking world into my system, I walk once more out to the truck. The first ten minutes of waking up are always the worst.

'It says it's a cardiac arrest, but reading the notes I wouldn't get too excited,' I say quietly as I scroll through the information on our data terminal. For a moment I'm distracted by the fuzziness of the letters and I try to blink my age away.

'I'll *try* not to get too excited,' my trainee replies. I recall the conversation we had at the beginning of our shift, which seems like weeks ago now. It turns out she also hates being awake in the early hours, so it is a shame that's when all the good work usually occurs.

The apparent cardiac arrest is in a laneway in Kings Cross, Sydney's red-light district and home to many hard-core drug addicts, junkies, hookers and homeless people. We do a huge amount of our work there, and it's impossible not to develop a soft spot for our clients and patients. At this hour it's really just the cops, the seedy nightlife and us.

A twenty-five-year-old female is in cardiac arrest. Knowing the area and knowing the time of day and knowing twenty-five year olds in these parts, I assume we're heading to an unconscious heroin overdose. And knowing the usual response from our treatment I wouldn't usually be concerned, but since the notes I've just read tell me there's a man on scene performing CPR, I'm a little concerned and press a little more firmly on the accelerator as we whiz through the intersections, lights and sirens ablaze. The undergoing of CPR is a sign that the patient is sick or looks sick. There is also the possibility that the dude doing the CPR is questionable, in which case my haste is about saving the patient from this bystander. Often many well-intentioned first aiders can cause unnecessary broken ribs and even 'slip in the tongue' to semi-conscious patients. With this in mind, I drive even faster.

'Negative on the cardiac arrest,' says the primary care crew who were first on scene, 'but keep the intensive care running.' A short and sweet report by the crew on scene breaks the silence in our truck as it crackles over the airwaves.

Just as I thought: a heroin overdose. I wonder how vigorous the CPR was! We're a few minutes behind the first crew and squeeze our truck through the dark back alleys of Kings Cross to meet up with them. A police vehicle blocks the road, and I shake my head quietly at their lack of foresight. My paramedic brain is already planning our quick exit from this roadside scene should we need to flee to the hospital in a hurry. Road blocks never help. Being absolutely exhausted and half asleep gives me a lazy mind, a mind that defaults to criticism a little too quickly.

A cool breeze greets me as I step out of the driver's side and make my way around to the side door. My partner is taking out the oxygen and I grab the drug kit. I know it's early in the morning because the bag feels twice its normal weight. It's a strange phenomenon, one that I curse often.

It's a typical scene of a Kings Cross laneway overdose: quiet and dark. I can see a body lying on its back, not moving, arms splayed out to the side. There's a man standing in the shadows watching the other crew working on the patient and I make a mental note of his size: huge. He's the only person here, so I assume he's the one who was performing CPR on this young woman. The cops are going through a handbag, tipping the contents all over the road. I can see the usual items such as tissues and chewing gum. I approach the body and the treating paramedics, who lift their heads as I greet them.

'Hi guys, what have you got there?' I ask, as a way to announce our arrival.

'Oh hi, Sandy, yeah, we found her here unconscious. Pretty sure it's a heroin OD. Her pupils are pinned, all the gear for shooting up is next to her here. We gave her a shot of Narcan and have been ventilating her for a few minutes. We were just about to give her another shot of Narcan.'

'Sounds good to me, here you go.' I reach into their open drug kit and pass the ready-made glass mini-jet of Narcan. These little beauties make our lives so much easier. The full dose of naloxone, which is sold under the brand name Narcan and is held in solution within a glass ampule, reverses the effects of a heroin overdose. There is a rubber plug at one end that is screwed into a syringe with a needle already attached to it. It takes around ten seconds to open the box, pop off the plastic caps, screw in the ampule to the syringe and eject any air. We then inject the drug straight into the muscle, generally in the thigh as it is always good and usually available. There is no need for multiple sharps, and the disused needle goes straight into the sharps container. Awesome.

God, I love competence, I think as I watch the junior ambos deal so well with this patient. They're doing everything: the airway is being guarded; the heart monitor is on showing a normal sinus rhythm; they've checked the patient's blood glucose. *What more could you ask for?*

It's no small feat either. These inner-city ambos have the whole routine down to a fine art. Some people say the inner-city work is second rate, but I beg to differ. With such a heavy volume of roadside trauma and unconscious drug- and alcohol-related cases, there is endless opportunity to perfect our basic skill set.

These basics are what make all the difference. Although we call this 'basic', it's really quite complex. The patient needs to be positioned in a way that doesn't worsen their condition. Imagine what would happen if they vomited ten glasses of champagne while unconscious on their back? That's right, not good. So the very first thing we do is roll them onto their side. Then we open up the gear and start applying various pieces of equipment to assist in breathing; and no, we do not perform mouth to mouth.

Once the patient is placed on their side, if they are unconscious we'll insert an oral or nasal airway. The oral one looks like a long, adult-sized dummy and holds the tongue out of the way. Sometimes the patient will be biting their teeth together so hard we can't open their mouth, so in such cases we insert a long plastic straw-like tube into their nose with the help of a decent squirt of slippery lube. It makes breathing easier. The downside of these nasal tubes is that they can cause nose bleeds. Unconscious patients are one thing; unconscious patients with gushing nose bleeds are another, but that's a different story.

With the airway now open, we assist the patient to breathe. Heroin affects the breathing centre; depending on how much the patient's had they can stop breathing altogether, in which case their heart will continue beating for some time but they'll turn a dramatic blue colour and sweat golf balls. Obviously, the breathing part is really important. We place a large, rigid mask over the nose and mouth that is attached to a large bag that looks like a football. It's filled with one hundred per cent oxygen via a tube and, when squeezed, forces oxygen into the patient. The mask seals the face, ensuring nothing leaks. It's clear when the oxygen has gone into the lungs as the chest will rise then fall. We press the bag every few seconds, imitating the natural breathing cycle, and in this way we effectively breathe for the patient. It takes one person to do this job properly, so the airway paramedic cannot multitask as they will always have their hands full.

The partner paramedic will be busy assessing the patient's status, cutting clothing or pulling it aside to attach electrodes to the shoulders and hips. Electrodes are little sticky dots with a jelly centre that make contact with the skin and feed information back to the Lifepak machine, an electrocardiogram that shows us the rate and rhythm of the heart. We can gather all sorts of information from this fantastic piece of gear. Costing about $15,000 a piece, the only downside is its weight – that ten kilograms – which is a little awkward to carry long distances but it is an absolute life-saving piece of kit. Our heroin overdoses can throw all sorts of exotic cardiac rhythms: tachycardias, where the heart is beating too fast; bradycardias, where the heart is beating too slow; and premature ventricular contractions, where the heart gets a little confused and throws in extra beats here and there throwing the rhythm off, just to name a few. There is almost always some sort of abnormality that occurs in the heart when there is profound oxygen starvation, and a heroin overdose will always cause that.

Once blood pressure is taken, it is usually time to test the blood sugar. We can do this by pricking the fingertip, then taking a drop of blood and feeding this into a small glucometer machine. It's quick, and we always do it, as a diabetic having a hypoglycaemic episode can present with erratic cardiac rhythms.

Next we then insert a cannula into an available vein. We start by placing a tourniquet around the upper arm, then cleaning the skin with an alcohol wipe. In dark alleyways a penlight is often our only source of light, and sometimes we hold this in our teeth to shine on the skin. The trouble with this method is that it makes the mouth water profusely and long strands of dribble can escape down the torch, but there's nothing we can do about it. The torch dribble never makes you look good; not only is it unhygienic, it's annoying and uncool. I find that the trusty headlamp alleviates this problem entirely, but I must confess I don't always take it with me. The penlight, however, is always in the front pocket.

Heroin addicts are notoriously difficult to cannulate. Their veins have been poked and prodded by way too many needles, and they sometimes have so much scar tissue build up you can hear cracking as the needle is forced through. But we will always try if the patient is sick enough to warrant one.

Gathering all this data is called 'taking observations' or 'obs'. We pass this information between us because not only does it dictate treatment, but it also brings all clinicians onto the same page. When we say that the patient is 'GCS [Glasgow Coma Scale] 3' we all know this means completely unconscious. It's a specific rating; the data speaks for itself, taking out any subjective bias. All this information is given to me, the intensive care back-up, upon arrival at the job.

On this particular job, I am impressed with the speed and skill of patient care and the gathering of obs by the primary care crew. Primary care means that the skill set is limited to the basics, but these guys are still trained to an impressive advanced life-support level. They are far from being 'basic' technicians. These days every single ambulance in New South Wales has a highly trained clinician on board.

Knowing that the second shot of Narcan is going to block all the opioid receptors in our patient's brain and make her wake up, I take a moment to speak with the man in the shadows to get more of an idea of what happened prior to our arrival. He's still standing there looking slightly panicked and pissed off. A cynical or perhaps just streetwise part of me is always cautious with these apparent helpers: I wonder if the patient's wallet has been cleaned out, if it was him who gave her the shot of heroin or if he might have been a little too intimate while practising his first-aid skills.

'G'day, mate, were you with her when she dropped?'

'Nah, I just fuckin' found her. Thought she was dead. I had to try and get her back, then the ambos arrived,' he replies.

'No worries. Well, thanks for doing that, you did the right thing there, always call us.'

Our unconscious patient should be waking up about now so I wander back over. As expected, she is taking big breaths. She hasn't opened her eyes though, and it seems we all notice the same thing simultaneously. The cop is the first person to say something, as he looks down at her with a furrowed brow.

'Um, is that right?' he questions, gesturing to her body position.

At once all eyes gaze upon her right arm, which has been hiding in the shadows of the night. It's shorter and fatter than it should be. It's the sort of arm you see on patients who are screaming in agony, yelling at you to hurry up and give them something to put them out of their misery.

What the? I think. My eyes grow wider as my brain tries to make sense of this picture. This arm is not part of the typical heroin OD picture. I am used to seeing this sort of thing with falls from a great height, car accidents and big trauma.

'Oh, looks like she's got a broken arm,' Janice, my partner, says to me rather wide-eyed.

Janice springs to life. She loves getting her hands on a decent injury and has an intimate knowledge of anatomy. She's kneeling next to me in a nanosecond, feeling the upper arm and giving us a blow-by-blow description of what she can feel.

'Oh wow, it's broken all right. I can feel crepitus. It's the humerus, seems to be articulating right in the middle.'

Janice is cradling the arm in her hands to support the injury, and her eyes glance up and slightly to the left as she continues her description. She's peering over her glasses as she speaks, looking like a scientist or a newsreader crouched down there. For a moment I think, *God, that would make a good photo.*

'I can feel the radius and ulna, no, it's the joint capsule.' She continues, but my mind has locked on her first description, 'crepitus'. This medical term describes the crunching and grating of bone that can be felt through the skin. There's no doubting it's crepitus, which is slightly gross at best and downright disturbing at worst to feel bones grinding away as they move like that.

The other term I heard was 'humerus', and I think to myself there must have been considerable force to break this bone. It is the long bone of the upper arm, with one end meeting the elbow and the other end the shoulder. My mind has just switched on to hyper-alert as I try and find possible causes for this trauma.

Oh dear, we don't have long, I think, immediately aware of the timeline, the fact that our patient is about to wake up and we've just reversed the effect of all opioid painkillers.

'Guys, she's got a broken arm, and we've just saturated her opioid receptors with all that Narcan. All the morphine in Sydney is not going to touch the sides with her! We need to splint her arm before she wakes up,' I say, rather a little too panicked for my liking.

I dash to the back of the truck to get the splint and padding. I rip bandages from their plastic wraps as I walk back to the patient, who is still lying on her back. We all spring into action to get the limb realignment over with before she wakes up; I know we only have seconds.

'Can you realign the limb and I'll slide this splint under her,' I say to one of the primary care paramedics. 'Janice, if you could prepare to wrap the splint up.'

I am now completely wide awake, barking orders in the hope we can prevent an absolutely torturous event for our patient. Watching her grossly deformed limb makes me squirm a little, and I'm grateful she's not fully alert for this. We tenderly place her upper arm in the splint, and I'm almost relieved at the thought we'll get this done before she wakes up. We just need to secure the splint by tying knots around the broad bandages.

We're seconds off securing her disarticulated arm into a state of alignment when, right at the moment of tying the first knot, our patient sits bolt upright and spits at us, launching a semi-crusty bubble of sputum into mid-air. It wobbles around as it makes a huge arc, but thankfully flies right over our heads. Her spit missile misses all of us, sticking to the side of the wall next to the police officer's head and beginning its lazy slide down.

'I did it two months ago, ya fuckin' mole!' she yells. She's like the horror movie Chucky, who just brought our worst nightmare to life. She pulls her arm out of our carefully padded splint and yanks it back to her side.

'Oh, you are fuckin' kiddin' me? Did youse give me Narcan? I'm gonna have to score again, *pricks!*' she screams, then launches another sputum projectile that hits the cop in the face. It is not a good thing to do, but we're in shock about the arm flinging around and barely react. Our reactions will come in the next few seconds, for sure.

We all take a step back and glance at each other with disbelief.

'What's your name?' I ask, as the cop wipes his face with the back of his gloved hand.

'Tammy! Fuck!' she says, and then spits on the ground.

'Well, don't move your arm, Tammy, it looks like it's going to fall off! We need to splint it,' I say.

Tammy is sitting in the gutter now trying to gather her belongings, which have been spread out. There is lip balm, chewing gum, screwed up pieces of paper and a fit kit. The cop sweeps them away from her reach with his foot and tells her to stop it. He is clearly pissed off.

My brain feels like it's not working. Tammy has the worst arm I've seen in a long time and yet she is throwing it round like a lasso.

Did that guy kneel on it? Was she run over by a car while she was out of it? I wonder.

'Tammy, I'm concerned about your arm,' I say. 'We really need to take you to hospital to get it looked at.'

'I'm telling you, it happened ages ago. I'm seeing the specialist tomorrow! I'm not fuckin' going to hospital and you can go fuck yourself,' she says with much more clarity and intent. Our friend is well and truly awake now.

The four ambos on scene are now standing and exchanging various looks of horror and incredulity. I give a little shrug.

'Righteo, Tammy, as long as you know we really think you should come with us and have it seen to. We could get you a cuppa and something to eat as well if you like, that arm looks terrible and should be treated now. I'm sure the specialist would agree.'

'Fuck you! Where's my stuff?' she shrieks at the cops.

Some might say that this scene right here is a loveless barren desert, as our patient is abusive and obnoxious. This scene is generating feelings in us that are far removed from love right now. Yet, despite this behaviour, both the police officers and paramedics present are deeply committed to offering a solution to this young woman. We see beyond the poor behaviour to the tragedy of a life that has led to chronic heroin addiction. Sometimes love takes the form of our actions in the face of conflicted feelings arising in us; sometimes love is a stern attitude and definitely a forgiving heart. Love is compassion and the capacity to see beyond the swearing and the spit to the suffering of the person within. Love is also good boundaries and respecting a person's right to decline our help, and our capacity to walk away in the hope that she gets better rather than hoping she gets what she deserves. Love never gives up on anyone and sees every breath as an opportunity to make a positive choice. Love steps in to protect when the person isn't lovable. Love helps other people without needed acknowledgement or a witness. Love is daring and sometimes humorous. Love understands that sometimes people need lifetimes to get their shit together.

Having exhausted all attempts at convincing this patient to come to hospital, we decide to leave her with the police. She's fully alert now yet not complaining of any pain; it's her choice whether she comes with us or not.

'Righteo, Tammy, we just need to check your pockets,' the police officer states.

'Don't fuckin' touch me!' Tammy yells, as she flings her broken limb wildly around.

The police try to restrain her, but she is so weirdly double jointed in that limb it's nearly impossible. It's as though they're trying to catch a snake.

I stand there dumfounded, glancing around at my colleagues who are sharing the same weird moment. All of us have furrowed brows and look aghast. We collect our debris of plastic wrap, bandages and the splint and put the gear back in the truck.

That was weird, I think, as I walk back to the truck. The others are putting stuff away, and I figure we can talk about how strange that job was when we next see them at hospital. I ponder how very like a child our patient is, throwing a tantrum and not listening to the annoying parents who know better. And so it is with so many children in adult bodies, people who have no idea how to care for themselves and on some level are completely out of control. The resistance, rebellion and craziness are all cries from the child within.

Love emerges in the provision of basic care and the enforcement of law. Tammy will probably not feel this law enforcement as love, but she would be dead if not for all of us involved; all she knows is the need for the drug and all we see is a life worth saving. And just as the perspective differs between parent and child, so too does ours here. It wasn't so difficult to see the wounded little girl behind those wild eyes, to forgive her and feel just a smidge of compassion.

So we interact briefly with this broken adult/child and take the full brunt of her venom. Of course, dodging spit balls is unacceptable to us and we have a policy of zero tolerance to violence, which can look to bystanders as though people are being restrained, arrested and sometimes charged with violence towards us and other emergency services. The question is, do we walk away filled with negative emotions and resentment, or do we walk away with compassion and tolerance?

Learning to find a greater capacity for unconditional love within my own heart has empowered me to release negative emotions. You know the ones: they encourage the inner cynic to bitch and moan about 'those people'. They can drag us down, and lead us into serious burn out.

I choose to believe that deep within everyone is a being looking for love. When people are cut off from love through life circumstances or personal karma, or whatever you want to call it, they can end up looking like our friend with the busted arm. Compassion asks me to see beyond the spit balls to the person suffering inside. I am no saint myself, but like most people I've indulged in poor behaviour at times and have suffered for it. So, really, who am I to judge?

As both a paramedic and a person in the world I cherish the well-being of others. I have a responsibility to appreciate their suffering and to do what I can to alleviate it. My soul has a bit of a hunger to take this quality as far as I can, which brings me to people who are difficult to love and gives me the opportunity to practise patience and tolerance and expand my capacity for love. When I'm in a fit spiritual condition I am quite conscious of this, and my thoughts sound a little like this: 'I know you want me to hate you and you are doing your best to do this, but I am committed to seeing you as innocent somewhere in there and I choose to love you anyway.'

My teacher once told me that 'every being responds to love', and I have never forgotten it. Love is my most powerful weapon, strengthening me against all kinds of negative feelings and helping me remember we are all imperfect beings in this imperfect world. That method may not work for everyone, but it certainly works for me.

So on this cold early morning, we respect this patient's right to refuse all help. We gather up our equipment and leave her with the police. She continues ranting and raving and making it difficult for the police to help her but our job ends here. We will probably cross paths with Tammy again as she scrapes the bottom of her barrel, so the very least I can do is not judge her and offer her some warmth, if only in my own heart.

8

AMAZING GRACE

*The timing of death, like the ending of a story, gives a changed meaning
to what preceded it.* – Mary Catherine Bateson

Ask any paramedic if there is any such thing as a 'good' death and
they will almost certainly say there is. We see the good, the bad and
the ugly in death; the stinky, the sad, the tragic and the graceful.

I have come to believe that death, like everything else, is a
matter of karma, that it is our grace and our karma that decide the
circumstances of our death. We're all at the mercy of the laws of the
universe, and the law of 'cause and effect' is karma: think a crappy
thought or do a harmful act and reap the negative consequences.
Maybe not on the same day or even in the same lifetime but, one
day, what goes around will come back around. I think of grace like an
offset account, that it offsets my negative karma.

The understanding of this became easier to comprehend when I
came to acknowledge that there is a part of ourselves – our spirit –
that is eternal, that exists long and far beyond this life. This part of
ourselves lives within each being lifetime after lifetime. This concept,
that the essential soul self has a long memory and sets the wheels of
karma in motion every single day, has helped me accept things as

they are. That we reap what we sow makes sense to me, as does: 'If you have a problem with what you're getting, look at what you're giving.' With the terrible things that happen to good people, it makes sense there is a dimension beyond the physical world in which life is perfectly balanced, but only if you consider life beyond the brief span of one lifetime.

The trouble for most of us is that we tend to view life from a relatively narrow and limited perspective, while I believe perfection can be found in a much broader perspective. When we focus our lens solely on one perspective, we may struggle to find the love. Once the lens relaxes and the aperture opens a little, love and perfection become much more apparent.

Karma can be positive or negative, the positive side of it being grace. Grace is our bank of blessings, our ultimate insurance policy. And we all want more of that, right? I imagine that every time I do something kind for someone, I throw a few coins in my grace account. When I forgive someone rather than hold on to hatred or resentment, a few more dollars go in. When I do service for other people, then more savings go in the grace account. I add to it as much as I can, because more and more I see the purpose of my life is to fill up this account. The more I focus on this, the better my life is. I consider myself graced beyond measure, and indeed I am.

I had the good fortune in this lifetime to have access to a great education, being schooled from ages four to seventeen in the Catholic education system. I then enjoyed a further four years at a Catholic university. I have fond memories of belting out hymns before class as we gathered for roll call in the chapel. Most of my gusto was for the pleasure of those around me, who I delighted in entertaining, but there was also a deep love for the structure and ritual this culture gave me. Something resonated deep within me at the thought of living a virtuous life. I had been hoping to find meaning somewhere, something to bring solace to a deep discord that lay within me.

When my education was complete I sought almost the opposite to a virtuous existence, practically to the gates of insanity and death. From the ages of twenty to twenty-five, the first five years of my career as a paramedic, I was as lost and broken as any of the saddest cases I served. I was just dressed up in an outfit that hid the truth from most. Living and working on life's knife edge, peering into the bleakness regularly, there were times I would have preferred to be dead.

I experienced moments of freedom from my torturous inner state on the dance floor and in various states of inebriation, but these moments were always fleeting and inevitably stolen by the dawning of a new day. The God of my childhood had long disappeared, and I was enduring my first dark night of the soul in this lifetime. It was in these years that I lost six friends to suicide and never questioned their decision to depart.

After a few major dramas and meltdowns, I reached that moment myself. Running late for work again, full of sickness and guilt and shame over things I couldn't even recall, the thought popped into my head: *I could end this all right now.* I looked at my watch and considered that I had just ten minutes to make up my mind or I'd miss signing on at work. I was at one of the lowest points of my life, tossing up whether to kill myself or go to work. I was fully lucid, rational and considered about it.

Some minutes passed, and the pressure of getting to work on time kicked in. I cursed, said *ah … fuck it*, launched myself out the door and headed in to work. I cannot recall much more of that day, only knowing that the gravity of the moment was lost to me, no doubt dissolved in the next beer and buried deep within.

At age twenty-five my life as I knew it was over. For various reasons it all caved in and my dear friend alcohol could no longer save me. In absolute desperation, I called out to a God I thought had long abandoned me, the simplest and most profound prayer of my life: 'God, help me.' Little did I know, that three days prior I had taken my last drink and complete redemption was about to dawn for me. Grace had entered my life through an opening of despair, and begun to saturate me. To this day, more than fifteen years later, that grace has never left me. My spirit returned to me, my inner light turned on, and I began to walk my path of happy destiny.

I discovered a spirituality that is not bound within a building or any other confines for that matter. I discovered the grace of an incredibly loving power and a method of connecting to that power. Every day since that moment, I have sought that connection and delighted in the miracles that spiritual source gives me.

It was quite a few years later that I realised how close to the edge I had stood and how apparent the grace in my life was. This and other experiences in my world have given me a perspective on grace that I may otherwise have not had. I have nothing but gratitude for those dark and difficult years, as they laid the foundation of a life that is now imbued with beauty and satisfaction beyond description.

So when I find myself among the architecture and artwork of a Catholic monastery or nursing home, my soul still feels quite at home. I was taught by nuns and ran from nuns at lunchtime in high school many times. The hymns we sang in school masses, coupled with the traditions, gave me a grounding in spirituality that made my soul feel like it had a place in the world.

There has always been a secret place inside me that loves to escape into the timeless stories and teachings of Christ. The aroma of frankincense sends me straight into an unknown yet familiar recollection of feeling at home in quiet corridors and soulful reflection. The heady aroma of sacramental wine alone seemed to change me even as a child.

Religious dogma has never been my thing, but I had a rich and wonderful introduction to spirituality thanks in part to my Catholic education. The train may have run off the tracks on some occasions and one or two people may have condemned me to hell, but the seeds of a strong faith were definitely sewn. I consider myself 'spiritual' as opposed to 'religious'. I have heard religion described as the 'politics' of God and spirituality the 'practice', and I like that definition. I am not one for politics, so I don't claim to be religious. Somehow I got through the ups and downs of my early years with a great yearning for spirituality. Perhaps it was in my soul already.

It is with a nostalgic heart that I enter St Theresa's Nursing Home for retired nuns. Familiar artworks depicting Mary MacKillop, Australia's first canonised saint, adorn the corridor and the scent of old wood fills the air. Wood and urine – this is, after all, a nursing home.

An incidence of gastroenteritis is why we've been called, but I can see this is not a simple case of 'nuns with the runs' when I look at Sister Catherine and receive the handover from the registered nurse.

'She is ninety-four, had gastro this afternoon then became so drowsy we could not wake her,' says the nurse in an Italian accent, with obvious concern for the patient, whom she thinks is 'septic'. Sepsis is a condition in which the entire system becomes affected by an infective process, then eventually the blood pressure and level of consciousness drop off and the patient can die. I can see how the nurse has made this diagnosis, as sepsis often looks like this. Sister Catherine may be septic, it's true, but either way she is not long for this world.

'Um,' I say with a furrowed brow as I glance at my partner.

'She looks pre-code four,' I say to my partner, attempting discretion by using our secret language. 'Code four' technically means 'call the cops, they're dead', but in this situation I know my partner understands I mean this nun is about to embark on her way to the pearly gates.

I get a slow nod in response and we all stand there waiting for someone to speak. I can tell by looking at this nun that she is in the process of dying. For a few reasons, like it or not, the bowels often relax just before death and tend to empty and, yes, this can easily be taken for gastro. That our nun is also breathing like a fish out of water is really not a good sign.

As her level of consciousness slips away, her breathing slows and changes rhythm. This is quite normal and predictable and, in cases where death is expected, no measures need be taken to assist breathing. Death comes knocking at all our doors in the fullness of time, and it seems to me all sanity is lost on those occasions when we are expected to perform a full resuscitation on a frail and elderly patient who is in the midst of a graceful departure.

After a chat out of earshot with my partner, we decide Sister Catherine needs to be transported to the emergency department. The nurse is now in a complete flap and disappears to photocopy paperwork.

Now, this is a tricky situation for us paramedics. There is an ethical debate around the dying process, and one could argue either way about whether it's appropriate to attempt to resuscitate this woman. She is at the end of her life and about to die a peaceful, almost dignified death – that is, until she finds herself in the hands of paramedics en route to an emergency department. We don't like arriving at a hospital with a deceased person, especially if they were alive before transport was commenced. When death occurs in the presence of paramedics, the case is reviewed to ensure no errors were made that contributed to the death.

In many cases, resuscitation is commenced and ceased at hospital in the presence of the medical team. Occasionally resuscitation will be commenced and ceased en route to hospital if it is obvious that treatment will be of no further avail, but for the most part resuscitation will continue all the way to hospital, despite the distance, the traffic or driving conditions. This being the case, it is easy to forgive the paramedic who makes a decision about where a person would prefer to die. If a person wishes to die at home and we can see death is imminent, it is frustrating to be pressured into transporting the patient to hospital then having to explain why they died in our company, or why we're performing aggressive resuscitation on a frail elderly person who is clearly at the end of their life.

There is a general implication that we will take actions to preserve life, no matter the circumstances. On rare occasions, an advanced care directive will have been put in place. This very important legal document gives the patient the option to choose what happens to their body during the dying process, specifying to what extent resuscitation is to be carried out. Sometimes, it is specified that all care and comfort be respected but no chest compressions administered or invasive airway inserted. It comes with great relief to know we can safely facilitate a peaceful passing en route to hospital and not fear we're doing something either legally or ethically wrong. For this reason, one of the first things we ask for when transferring a dying patient from a nursing home to the emergency department to die is the advanced care directive. Unfortunately, however, nine times out of ten there is no documentation, mostly because the family is not happy to discuss these issues and so 'wants everything possible done', which from our perspective often seems completely inappropriate and even barbaric.

In a perfect world, our beautiful little nun (she's tiny, actually) would die in her own bed to the sound of Gregorian chants with a loved one at her bedside – death is such a vulnerable time. But there is no perfect world, as paramedics will often tell you.

With the nurse stressing out for whatever reason and no directive to be found, the assumption is that we will do everything for this patient. We approach her tenderly, reassure her then load her onto the stretcher then into the ambulance. She doesn't startle as we slide her onto the stretcher, letting out a faint yet audible noise. We exchange her soft pink doona for our white blankets, and I pop an extra one on her as she feels a little cool to touch.

We transport beautiful Sister Catherine to the emergency department; I can see there are only precious minutes remaining. Just as you cannot push a baby back up a birth canal, you can't prevent a soul from leaving the body when it is time to go home. For the twenty-minute journey to hospital, I do my best to keep her comfortable and warm. I offer words of comfort and reassurance, oxygen blowing gently into her nose. I place a cardiac monitor on her and keep a close eye on the rhythm, hoping and even praying that she hold on for now. Thankfully the moment does not arrive while we are on the way to the hospital, but as we pull up at triage I know the time has come.

The nurse is doing the million things a triage nurse does at a busy hospital front desk. The word triage means to sort; a senior nurse takes this role at the emergency department and sorts the patients as they present. Each patient is given a category of severity that reflects the timeframe in which the patient needs to be seen. Urgent, life-threatening cases are seen immediately; less urgent cases are seen after. This is a great system as it means you cannot jump the queue, something people try to do frequently by calling ambulances. We will politely explain that the triage system ensures patients are seen according to their medical need rather than to the means of transport they take to the hospital.

I gesture that I will stand by our patient's side while my partner passes on the details to the triage nurse. I really don't want to leave her side at this moment. The instinct that drives me to stand close to her is not based on any belief that my treatment will prevent her deteriorating or dying; it feels more like a need to let her sense my presence. I know I can offer her a calm presence, and this feels good. I am completely comfortable with the fact she is dying; she is so old and frail it seems right to let her go.

Now that we are inside the hospital, it seems easier to hand the patient over as 'in the dying process' rather than 'she died en route', which is a little silly, really, and perhaps a sign of rules having gone rigid. Nevertheless, the nurse takes one look at Sister Catherine and sees what I see. At no point is there an assumption that we will start to resuscitate, rather that we find a private place for these last moments to take place. The nurse picks up the internal phone to organise a room for us to move her in to and gestures 'one minute' with her hand. I nod in response to this acknowledgement of what is taking place.

And so, here I am with Sister Catherine. As far as I know I have never met her before nor she me, but as fate or grace would have it I am the person right by her side at this time. I gently stroke her cheek and forehead, and brush strands of hair from her eyes. She has no control over her body and is not moving but her breathing is a little laboured. She is very frail, and I wonder what adventures she has had in this life. She has devoted her life to God and her faith, an almost unfathomable level of devotion to me. I feel a little sad for her, that she is in this clinical environment under fluorescent lights amid the drama and noise of a big hospital. Of course, my sense that something is wrong here is the perspective of the narrowly focused lens. It seems ridiculous that this is even happening, and wrong that this frail patient, clearly at the end of a long life, is being rushed to the emergency department for this moment.

'Close your eyes, Sister Catherine, rest your mind, you are safe,' I say to her as I continue to offer a gentle, caring touch. I am fully aware her spirit is leaving her body. In this moment the fluorescent lights and public space feel inappropriate, but other than that this is a beautiful, peaceful experience.

Vomit starts emerging from her mouth and right in the nick of time we get the go-ahead to take her in to a hospital bed. She passes away within moments, taking her last breath as we move her onto the hospital bed. There are four of us with her for this moment, two paramedics and two nurses. It is obvious she is gone. We all look at her, exchanging no words, just watching the last sparks of life leave her little body. Interestingly, not once is there a mention or an attempt to resuscitate. I am quietly relieved that we are all on the same page here, that a peaceful passing is okay.

Grace is such a powerful force that can manipulate all sorts of factors to ensure the best in any situation. Perhaps it was grace, the timing of Sister Catherine's death. Perhaps it was grace that ensured she was surrounded by medical staff who were comfortable with letting her die peacefully.

'Oh, that's sad,' says a nurse with an Irish accent as she whisks out of the room.

Silently I call on the nun's spiritual team who love her unconditionally and say a prayer that she be guided home to her world of spirit. I am left with a sense of humility and gratitude for this experience, that I could play my small part for this soul.

There is a sense of perfection around Sister Catherine's passing. I believe nothing happens by mistake, and I am aware of much grace within this devout woman of God. This may not appear to be much: on the outside, the job looks incredibly frustrating, dealing with a nursing home that is clearly unprepared to deal with the expected passing of an elderly, unwell patient. To the untrained eye, it could look like a meaningless transport that we should not have had to do. However, to the love-trained eye it is a perfect demonstration of grace: had we not taken Sister Catherine she would have died alone. Had we not been there, she may not have been in the company of an understanding person who offered prayers right at the moment of her passing.

If you take away the external details and focus on the moment of her death, it was splendid. Perhaps it was her grace that ensured that she got the love, attention, peace, support and prayers she wanted at the moment she died. She may have hoped for it, but never imagined it would come from a paramedic. But still, love, peace and support came. Paramedics are frequently earth angels for the dying; for many people, the last look, last helping hand, and last expression of love comes from a paramedic.

Sometimes I wonder if perhaps some grace has accumulated within my own soul. If the soul exists in a dimension free from linear time constraints, then maybe the lives I've helped save and the deaths I've prevented or assisted all helped me in my own moment of choice. A spilt-second decision that day to go to work to help others may have saved my life and prevented a very sad death indeed. I can't imagine not being here now. Thank God I didn't make the decision to go, as it would have been a long-term solution to a short-term problem. I have lived the most extraordinary life, and I believe the best is yet to come. And to think, the fear of running late for work was the thing that changed my mind. Grace presents itself in the most unexpected ways.

 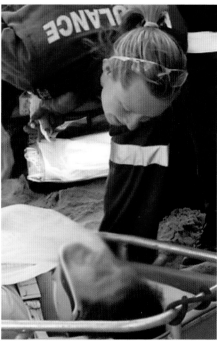

We work alongside the police and fire rescue alike. There is nothing quite like the feeling of working well together in a multi-disciplinary team.

A safe and happy patient about to be extricated from a beach after a fall from a cliff.

Rescuing Mandy the greyhound. There is something to be said about a society that values the welfare of animals as highly as it does that of humans.

Nestled in between my feet is a woman who had fallen down a narrow gap between a retaining wall; it was a lengthy process removing the bricks one by one to eventually free her.

Enjoying a moment with the hosts of morning TV program Sunrise. Resuscitating a dog won the hearts of many and created a huge amount of attention.

The Philippines, shortly after typhoon Yolanda hit. Taking a break from the clinic with a walk around the block.

Incomprehensible damage to the coastal villages near Tacloban, in the Philippines. Super Typhoon Yolanda, one of the strongest ever recorded, killed thousands of people in 2013.

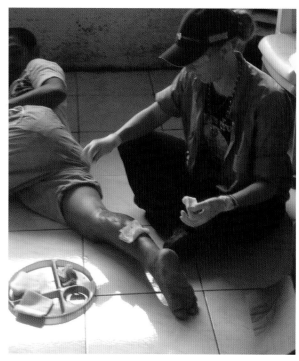

My section of the clinic, which was dedicated to wound cleaning. We had plastic food trays for equipment and dressings and provided as much comfort as we could on a hard tiled floor. We treated hundreds of people, who all waited patiently to see us; not one person complained about anything at any time.

A huge ship sits on the main road in Tacloban, high and dry after being pushed out of the water on the storm surge. The typhoon generated the equivalent of a tsunami, the power of which is evident here.

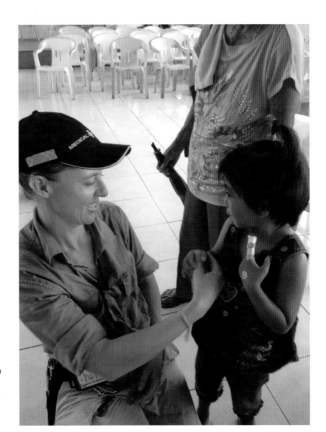

Perhaps the most resilient people I have ever met, it was a privilege to be of service in the Philippines. The children were the first to bring a spark of life back to many, I think.

Beginning our journey home from the Philippines. Although the fatigue is written all over my face, it was a moment of deep peace and satisfaction.

For me, spirituality and meditation are about being authentic and real and unleashing your inner joy.

Standing at 6,400 metres on the summit of Mera Peak in the Himalayas, Nepal. Some of the greatest adventures of my lfe have been found in the restful moments of annual leave from the job.

I have found that having a balanced life that includes not only physical fitness, but spiritual practice, keeps all facets of me in tip top condition.

Running a women's retreat in Sydney's Blue Mountains six months pregnant.

Leadership development is another area that draws on the skills of both the paramedic and the spiritual teacher. I love presenting to community and corporate groups.

Since 2015 I have run two classes a week on meditation and spirituality.

9
TAKING THE FALL

Life is what happens to us while we are making other plans.
– Allen Saunders

For a paramedic working throughout the silly season, it can feel like one tragedy after another. Attending cases that involve trauma and death in a time that is supposed to be about celebration and family only compounds the complex grief we may be carrying.

As paramedics the grief of others is not really ours, but we still feel it. We empathise with the pain of those we treat; how can we not? We're human: we too have loved ones and we too celebrate, and while doing so occasionally do stupid things that have unintended consequences. We understand that the hopes and dreams of happiness can be shattered in a moment, and life will never be the same again.

When alcohol is involved and someone makes a stupid choice that creates a whole mess, it is tragic. Some may argue that, like so many other alcohol-related incidences, this particular accident was preventable – and it probably was. But the fact remains the person took the drink, the drink affected their decision and tragic consequences were the result.

Despite the tragedy, we still dwell in the ambo mind: when there is

113

a big job, we want to be there. We run towards situations that terrify most people, knowing full well what emotional intensity awaits us. Knowing we have the capacity to assist in these situations, to restore a semblance of order from the chaos, feels good.

When this particular job is aired over the radio, our truck and every other truck in the local area hears the call. Suddenly all those ambulance resources that are busy refuelling, restocking, handing over at hospital, cleaning equipment or completing paperwork become available, including us.

'Ah, nine-eighty-one Sydney, we are five minutes from that accident, would you like us to attend?' I say over the radio, feeling that familiar urgency to attend the major trauma case that has just been announced.

'Thanks nine-eighty-one, I'll send you as the back-up, we have a local resource currently arriving on scene,' comes the reply.

'Copy that, nine-eighty-one is responding priority one to the long fall,' I respond in a monotone, muting any obvious excitement I am feeling to be on what most would consider a decent job, a time-critical medical emergency requiring intervention, careful consideration, extrication and clinical treatment.

'Thanks nine-eighty-one,' dispatch responds. We're on it, I can relax, all is right in the world of paramedicine: the intensive care crew is on the intensive care job, and in this moment that's all that matters. It's not that there isn't great satisfaction in non-emergency work; there is. The fact is most of the cases we attend are not time-critical emergencies, so when a case like this comes along I want to jump at it.

There is something deeply satisfying knowing that a patient is about to receive attention from people who are ready and capable of dealing with their problems. Conversely, it can be frustrating responding to an absurd call such as 'my electric blanket is too hot' while a real emergency goes down, leaving us unavailable.

With a 'nine' prefix on our ambulance, depending on the case we have a slight advantage as the nine distinguishes an intensive care paramedic resource. Typically we are used for the more urgent and life-threatening cases. Intensive care or IC paramedics are highly skilled and equipped to take the emergency room to the patient. With life-saving drugs and procedures, this resource is crucial in life-threatening situations: we can keep the patient alive long enough to get them to the hospital emergency department.

We paramedics have a few life-saving procedures up our sleeves that will save a patient's life if carried out in those crucial pre-hospital minutes. We can perform invasive procedures such as chest decompression, which involves inserting a large needle into the chest to re-inflate a collapsed lung, or intubation, an advanced form of airway management usually performed under general anaesthetic. We perform intra-osseous access in children when veins have collapsed, a process that involves firmly inserting a long needle directly into bone marrow, like a nail in a board, to allow fluids to enter. We can also provide various drug therapies.

In critical cases we need to perform these interventions immediately to preserve life. There are certain situations in which, if left untreated in the pre-hospital setting, the patient will most certainly die. There are two phrases we throw around with regard to critical patients – 'stay and play', and 'load and go' – and in some situations making the wrong call will result in death. Perhaps the most valuable assets we have as more senior clinicians are time in the job and experience. It takes confidence and wisdom to be able to fight the urge to bolt to hospital when a life-saving procedure needs to be done in the field with caution and precision. Likewise, it takes humility and a capacity for lateral thinking and broadmindedness to be able to change a treatment plan or even withhold certain treatment you might be comfortable with in order to prioritise timely transport to hospital where, for example, surgery might be urgently required.

Ours is an incredibly stressful job, but paramedics tend to experience the stress as job satisfaction rather than conventional stress. We reach a heightened state very quickly, but you wouldn't typically see us appearing to be stressed. Usually we are calm, polite, orderly and even humorous. I cannot say for sure if our sense of humour is actually funny to anyone else; there are certain twists and kinks within our psyche that make us laugh at the most ridiculous things. Such stories are shared among our own, in full appreciation of the need to laugh sometimes, perhaps so we can cope. There is also the indescribable absurdity of some cases, which only a paramedic could appreciate.

And so to the Christmas drinks disaster. As fate would have it, this particular job gets two 'nine' trucks attending. Three out of the four paramedics are intensive care specialists, which means there are many years' experience among the team.

I am the driver today and there is already a crew on scene with the patient, so my key role will be to ensure the ambos treating the patient have everything they need. I will also have to keep an ear on the radio and give reports from the scene to the dispatch centre, and prepare the stretcher and carrying devices for the extrication.

People often ask us about driving, tending to assume we must get road rage and frustration when dealing with the snarly Sydney traffic, but it's not really the case. Despite the serious nature of this job and our obvious enthusiasm, both my partner and I step into the ambulance with what looks like no great urgency. You'll never see an ambo run, unless it's to cross the road to pick up a coffee! Rushing creates a flustered state, and it's difficult to make important decisions in a state of angst. There is no point yelling at the traffic; when it clears we move through it. We arrive in a state of calm, which helps things flow smoothly and enables us to ease the fears of others.

The details come down on the data terminal screen and I check the address. I am fairly certain I know this street, but to make sure I can get there quickly with no navigational errors I load the address into my GPS and view the map. I pop a piece of gum in my mouth and put on my sunglasses. We then drive slowly out of the hospital to the first intersection and hold off on the siren for a few blocks, out of respect for the hospital staff and patients.

'So what happened with your renovations?' I ask my partner. 'Did the plumber make it around this week?' I'm following up on a conversation we started earlier in the day. We glide through the first intersection with the normal flow of traffic.

'Oh, you wouldn't believe it,' he responds. 'They put the job off again! The bathroom is like a bloody war zone, and Annie is absolutely losing her shit over it.' He shakes his head, clearly frustrated.

As we head along the Pacific Highway and out of earshot of the hospital, I turn on the siren and the beacons. We are lit up like a Christmas tree and everyone within one hundred metres can hear us. I move to the outside lane and step on the accelerator, and we zoom through the traffic as our speed builds.

'No way, how annoying!' I say. 'God, your poor wife. Is your youngest walking yet?'

'Clear left,' my partner says, alerting me to the fact that he has looked left as we pass through the intersection and it is clear of traffic.

'Ta,' I acknowledge, and proceed through the intersection against the red light, again building my speed to continue passing slower traffic.

'That's the bloody annoying thing, she just started walking and is getting into everything so she is always sneaking into the bathroom, ending up with dust and junk all over her,' he says. 'Clear left.'

'Thanks,' I respond. 'That's so irritating. Are you going to stay with this plumbing company, mate?' I ask, as I drive straight over the median strip. I slow down a little, as I'm driving on the wrong side of the road now. Cars see us coming and reduce their speed as they merge out of our way. The siren alternates between its long drone sound and a more high-pitched yelp. It's loud, but with the windows up we can still perfectly well hear each other talk. To my ears, the siren is not really loud; my brain must know how to drown it out.

'Annie went to school with the plumber and feels all guilty about getting up him for taking so long,' my partner says. I shake my head a little, knowing his wife Annie well enough and worrying that she might be getting taken advantage of here. We're whistling along Military Road and come up to another intersection and I'm looking to my right for vehicles so I can move us through a red light.

'No, not yet, not yet, no, still not clear,' my partner says in a calm voice.

I edge the ambulance through the intersection and wait for all lanes of traffic to respond to our movements, either stopping or pulling aside.

'Stop!' My partner calls a little louder as I step hard on the brake, pushing us both into our seatbelts. Out of the blue a large four-wheel drive flies past us, the driver, a young woman, talking on her phone. When she sees us her eyes turn large, and she gestures a 'sorry' and drives right by.

'Fuck!' my partner yells.

'Idiot!' I say under my breath, as I continue driving down this major roadway.

A surge of adrenaline dumps into my gut and I discharge as much as possible through my one word curse. It's a momentary fright, but my mind moves on quickly as we face the demands of the traffic. A near miss with a bus distracts me from my judgemental thoughts about the woman on her phone, and within moments we're back into our conversation.

'Yes, well, I guess you guys know what you're doing, but if you need another plumber you could always use Trevor. You know he's a plumber?' I say.

'Yeah, I considered Trev. We will see how this guy goes and change if we have to,' my partner says.

'Okay, mate, sounds good. Hey, I'll run the back streets at the top of Spit Hill, okay?'

'Yes, sure. Do you need me to direct you?'

'No thanks, I know the back streets.'

We lurch over the median strip again, and a long stretch of clear road lies ahead of us. I step on the accelerator and we fly down the road. With just a minute or less to go before we arrive on the scene, our conversation naturally winds down. My partner reaches for a spare set of gloves and places them in his glove pouch.

'Can you please get me some small gloves?' I ask.

He pulls them out like tissues from a box and I shove them into my pocket. I switch the siren off as we pull into the street, but the beacons are still flashing and I can see police cars lined up – always a good indicator of a successful navigation.

I double park outside the address, pretty much blocking all traffic, but our priority is accessing the patient. The police can move our truck later if necessary. If it were the scene of a fire I would probably leave the keys in the ignition and the engine running with the beacons on, which makes it easier to deal with road blocks when multiple agencies are attending the same job.

My first impression as we enter the premises is 'they're loaded'. It's a huge mansion overlooking spectacular Sydney Harbour. We enter through the front door and find a wide-eyed woman speaking to a bunch of kids in a bath. I can see she is anxious and distressed but adopting a motherly role, telling a group of at least three young children to stay where they are. She is direct and firm and I look past her: the children in the bath appear to be well, calm and quite relaxed and happy to follow her commands.

'I don't want the kids to know what's happened,' she says to me in a hushed voice. She gently pushes another child, perhaps aged ten, into the bathroom and says to her: 'Read the children a story, darling, keep them in there.'

'Can you please take me to where the other paramedics are?' I say in a calm voice, already adopting a tone and demeanour that lets her know we are here for her as well as for our patient.

'Oh my God, he's over the balcony on a ledge,' she says. 'Oh, I think he's broken his neck! Don't let the kids know! Oh shit! He's over here.'

'Thank you, and can I ask what is your relationship to the patient?'

'I'm his wife,' she responds, in shock.

'Okay, and what's your name, love?'

'It's Sue. I'm Sue. Sorry, hi,' she answers, smiling politely. The house and her manner make me think the family is educated and in well-paid work. There is even more money on the walls in the form of art. The view is spectacular, and crystal vases overflow with hundreds of dollars worth of flowers: lilies, exotic palms and roses decorate the living room. Toys are strewn all over the floor in the kids' bedroom and I get a sense that social time for this family would involve a lot of laughter, wine and happy background noise. The atmosphere must have been very 'happy family', and the thud of my work boots on the polished floorboards adds to the ominous vibe we bring with us. 'Major drama in otherwise awesome family life' is the situation here.

With a few police crews on scene already, this typically happy family Christmas party has just turned into a major combined emergency services event.

'Hi Sue, I'm Sandy, just slow your breathing a bit,' I say. 'Let's go have a look,' I add, with a warm smile. Body language and communication play a huge role in these moments; as the world is spinning completely out of control for those involved, words of encouragement and simple instruction help people to navigate.

We walk through the house, and I cannot help but be drawn to the dramatic view. The lounge room is huge and gorgeous. We walk past a balcony that has bottles of what look like expensive wines balancing on the balustrade. Large, half-full glasses sit unattended next to a cheese platter; the smell of cooked meat permeates the air, although I cannot see a barbecue.

It looks like the perfect place to celebrate the Christmas season with friends. The air is warm, and the light breeze offers a sweet coolness in the hot summer twilight. I approach the balcony and move all the glasses to the side. This is no longer the scene of a party but a medical rescue, and all hazards must go. We remove the cheese platter from the table, which now makes a perfect loading zone for our multiple bags of equipment and radios. I am moving shoes out of the way, clearing the walkway completely.

I peer over the balcony and there he is, three metres down on the roof of a garage made of large aluminum ridges. A middle-aged male is lying on his back with a cervical collar in place, conscious but with his arms and legs motionless. My colleagues, two of the best, are at his side working. They're inserting an intravenous cannula in the crook of his arm, preparing medication and fluids and taking clinical observations.

'Hi guys, we're here now, do you need anything?' I call out to the ambos below.

'Hello, Macken!' pipes one of the treating paramedics, my friend, Dave. 'Lovely to have you along. I think we're right here, but if you would be so kind as to pass down a towel, my knees are killing me!'

'Sure, Dave,' I respond, resisting the temptation to remark on his age.

'Oh, and a report mate, can you do us the pleasure? We've got a confirmed spinal injury, mate. We'd really love to airlift our friend out of here.'

'Copy, I'll be back shortly,' I reply.

Right. Well, that's shit! Here's a guy who doesn't look that sick: he's a good colour, his eyes are open and he's staring straight ahead. He is not screaming in agony, indeed, not even complaining – or moving, for that matter.

We all know how bad it is, those two words, 'spinal injury', saying it all. Chances are the patient will never walk again. It's when this information comes through that we all know, without saying anything more, that we're dealing with a major trauma with potentially catastrophic consequences. We can assume that the fractures in his neck, severe enough to damage the spinal cord within, are unstable. One move, even a millimetre, and that cord could sever, which could stop his breathing or do further damage to his nervous system. We need to do this job with the utmost precision and patience, and with as little movement as possible. The problem is, he's lying on a roof.

It turns out this lovely guy, loved by his friends and family, had been pretending to dangle one of the kids over the edge of the balcony. He'd had a few Christmas drinks, and he accidentally dropped her over. As he realised she was slipping from his grip he panicked and tried to strengthen his grip, but his reactions were too slow and the little girl fell. He leapt after her, at the mercy of the laws of physics. Gravity pulled him down and he couldn't control the consequences now set in motion. In a split second a part of his body collided with the little girl, altering her impact on the roof. She rolled, and he crashed. He took the load of the fall on his head, shattering every bone and intervertebral disc in his neck. The little girl was safe, but he cannot feel anything from the nipples down. The girl was lifted back up to the balcony before we arrived, but her favourite, friendly and usually funny uncle is lying very awake and completely motionless below.

When more information comes to light and we discover that the girl in question is the one babysitting the children in the bath, I immediately assess her and have another ambulance respond urgently to the scene. Although she seems okay she has fallen three metres, and we'll treat her with urgency as well. She is a delightful ten year old, mature beyond her years and absolutely terrified for the safety of her silly Uncle Toby. Through some remarkable twist of fate, she is apparently uninjured.

And so the job unfolds. Slowly we work into the night to secure our patient and devise a safe extrication plan. He's in an awkward spot on a garage roof, so this is time consuming and involves the fire-rescue team rigging up ropes and pulley systems to move him safely once he's placed in a Stokes litter (a cage that fully immobilises a patient before being carried over tricky terrain).

The patient has an IV cannula in his arm and intravenous fluids are running. One of the complications of such an injury is spinal shock, which causes the blood pressure to fall. Our patient has severe pain shooting into his arms, and Dave is doing a great job of managing his pain with multiple repeat doses of morphine. It becomes a fine balance, as we need to manage both pain and blood pressure. Opioids affect blood pressure, so we need to observe him closely and adjust the IV fluids to counterbalance these changes in his system. We have other drugs for pain relief, of course, but these too have side effects that could be detrimental to a spinal cord injury. The last thing we need is a ketamine-induced muscular response or a distressed patient, so in this scenario I respect Dave's decision to stick with morphine.

As well as a cervical collar around his neck, we place the patient on a hard spineboard and strap him in. We then need six people to lift him up on this board and place it within the Stokes litter. The cage has a small wall around it roughly twenty centimetres high, and the patient is lashed into it so he doesn't slide up or down. It is nearly impossible to keep a patient entirely flat during a difficult extrication, so this lashing is vitally important. We use rope for this part.

We have the patient under blankets to preserve body temperature and we've placed an oxygen mask on his face, as narcotics suppress breathing to a degree. At the end of all this preparation he is quite the bundle. Including all the equipment, we're looking at about 150 kilograms that we have to lift. It will take at least eight people to carry him to the waiting ambulance stretcher, along a fifty-metre route.

We are well into the second hour with the patient and his family before we depart. There is no helicopter available to assist us, so road transport will have to do. It is dark now and there is a full complement of about twenty emergency workers here – multiple crews of police and fire brigade and ambulance personnel. Carrying the patient is awkward and involves us lifting him over a ten-metre drop. The path is lit by bright torchlight, which is both a blessing and a curse. One glance into that light and anyone of us could be blinded for the next five minutes, with every subsequent step made into an abyss of blackness.

We take it in turns to support each other as we step the packaged patient over the tricky parts. Everyone is watching out for everyone else and we work together, step by step, to move him off the roof and into the neighbour's garden through a hole in the fence that the fire brigade created by cutting planks, then up what may well be Sydney's steepest driveway.

I get the job of transporting Sue, the patient's wife, to the emergency department once our patient has been loaded. Like everyone else on this job, she has been a walking, talking example of courage; now it's time for an important chat.

She wants details and it's my duty to be frank with her. I'm ready for her questions. 'What's the worst possible outcome?' she asks reluctantly.

'Sue, the worst possible outcome as far as I can tell would be spinal damage,' I tell her. 'If this is the case, Toby's movement and control of his body will be impaired.' It's not easy to say this, but it is the clinical truth. If I were in this situation I would want the facts too, so I decide to pass on all the information I have.

We each have different ideas of what it means to have a spinal injury, but it usually means never walking again. It means never working your normal job and being dependent on others for the rest of your life. It usually means never surfing or swimming again. It means life as we know it is over.

From my perspective, I need to assist this woman to start processing the information. I intuitively know how much detail to give to help her without overwhelming her. This is a case-by-case scenario: when family members are in shock, distressed and difficult to manage, this part of the job would entail calming talk only. I would give very simple instructions, emotional and sometimes physical hand holding all the way to the emergency room. But Sue is grounded, calm and courageous, and it seems as though she's really stepping into the role of the strong one for her family.

'Oh my God, this is so ironic, he is usually the strong one, he can do anything!' she says. 'I cannot believe this is happening to him. Oh, if you only knew!' She has the big picture of their life's journey together.

I know exactly what she's talking about. When the soul needs to learn something it doesn't really mind how it learns, just that it does. If someone has always been the strong one, never risking vulnerability, refusing help and remaining independent, then sometimes life intervenes and we enter the learning zone.

We can argue that life is cruel and unfair, and this accident might certainly be a case of a bad thing happening to good people. But where does that get us? Straight to miserable victim land, that's where. And what about the flip side? Here is someone telling me that she doesn't play the strong one in this relationship, and I get the sense the tables have just turned.

So it is with soul contracts, those unmistakable bonds between people that pull us together to help us learn and grow. Just when you think you're not capable of stepping into your life in a certain way, something happens and life demands that you step up. And what do you discover? You can actually do that thing you thought you never would, that your soul is hungry for the challenge with which those dramatic circumstances present you.

So often it is these very circumstances we would never wish upon anybody that open us up in ways we never thought possible. There are stories of people tapping into superhuman strength to lift vehicles that are trapping people underneath, powers that were never available in day-to-day life. As I watch this scene unfold, I can see the telltale signs of souls in action. I sense that Sue will be tapping into her own personal super powers for her husband through this ordeal; I can see her doing it already.

'Sue, I know it is all really overwhelming right now but can I just say something?' I ask.

'Yes, sure,' she responds, desperate for answers.

'All you have to do is today,' I tell her. 'That's it. Let's just break it down to bite-sized chunks. Right now, all you need to do is sip on your water there and keep breathing, and when we get to the hospital hold Toby's hand and tell him you are right there with him. That's it. Does that sound possible?'

'Yes, yes, it does.'

'Okay, that's the plan then,' I say in a calm, matter-of-fact way.

'Okay, that's the plan,' Sue repeats, relaxing her shoulders a little. She exhales a long sigh. Then I feel her mind kick in and she is back in panic mode.

'What then?' she asks. 'How are we going to manage this?'

'You'll be assisted with the next thing when it happens,' I say. 'We will help you and the hospital staff will help you through every step of the way. Remember, all you have to do is what is immediately in front of you.'

She seems all right with this plan. It's the best I can come up with in the moment, but I can see ahead. I've treated enough quadriplegics and I know all about the complications, the difficulties and the all-consuming life changes that occur. I know the chances are high that Toby will never move his body again.

I also know that this woman seems capable and courageous but doesn't quite know it yet. I know they will get through this, because they have to get through this.

Our patient, although arguably drunk and foolish, did an incredibly courageous thing. The moment that he realised he had dropped that little girl, he threw himself straight over to protect her. Two people fall from a balcony and one ends up with a spinal injury; the little girl has not even sustained a bruise. She is devastated that he's injured, and seems wise beyond her years as she processes the event. Perhaps he did save her, perhaps his actions caused a correction of that stupid drunk joke, and in doing so the negative consequences of the accident fell onto him.

I like to be aware of the laws of the universe in processing jobs like this. Life often doesn't make sense, or it doesn't seem fair until I pop on another lens through which to view it. Take, for example, the law of cause and effect, or karma, in which every action has an equal and opposite reaction. Now, let's presume the soul is the eternal part of us, that it has existed since before we were born and has accumulated both positive and negative credits for actions taken over many lifetimes. If we accept this, 'fair' doesn't have a legitimate

128

place in the argument. We are all simply experiencing our own cause and effect.

But it's not all bad. I imagine that grace, or divine assistance, is intertwined with karma. If you look hard enough, you'll start to see it too. Just ask yourself if anything positive has come from your own challenges. Are you stronger, or more independent? Have you had an opportunity to practise forgiveness? Have you had the opportunity to grow? In my experience, when I allow difficult circumstances to shape me into a better person that sense of grace seems to multiply. I experience life in a very dynamic way.

I like to think that hidden somewhere in this tragedy is the mark of love, and I sometimes still think about this beautiful family as there was such a likeable quality about them. I like to think that Sue will come to know herself as a pillar of strength and that Toby, well, maybe he took one for the team on this occasion. Who knows? Our situations and circumstances, good and bad, provide us with all the opportunities we need to make choices, to learn and grow.

Often times our deepest learning comes wrapped up in the strangest parcels. If we take each moment as it comes, one breath at a time, as best we can, then it all turns out in the end. A crazy, pear-shaped mess we find ourselves in can turn out to be the very thing that delivers us the magic moments our souls so desire.

10

LOVE'S TRAGIC BOND

*Ever has it been that love knows not its own depth until
the hour of separation.* – Kahil Gibran

'Nine-eighty-four on the air please, nine-eighty-four.' The intercom
awakens and pulls us all from our semi-slumber. It's hardly sleeping,
though; it's called 'downtime': time to lie down, wind down and
recharge. This precious time we sometimes get between jobs allows
the nervous system to recover and the mind to switch off. The
problem with falling into a deep sleep is that the wake-up call jolts
your system, giving a frightening return of the senses. We learn to
sleep with a part of us always awake ready to answer the call, ready to
switch on, be present and professional within moments. So we wait,
knowing that somewhere out there something tragic or traumatic is
about to happen. It may be in three hours or three minutes, but soon
we will play our part in the life-changing event of someone else's life.

I've been curled up on the couch, drooling into starchy
white hospital sheets as they drape messily over the ambulance
station furniture. It's an etiquette thing: nobody likes the idea of
contamination, so our work clothes shouldn't touch the furniture.
We pick up things that stick to our shoes; sometimes it's dog poo

and sometimes it's human poo. That's only the stuff we can see; God knows what else we pick up as we walk through the lives and deaths of the public we serve: the good, the bad and everything in between.

Before I even begin to think my feet are walking me to the ambulance, which by now will be cold and sitting idle in the parking bay. My weary state tells me we've been dozing for at least an hour, maybe more. It's cold as I walk outside, and my body protests just a little as the chill nips my fingers and nose.

There is something in the tone of the dispatcher's voice that tells me to move fast on this one. Perhaps it's my intuition, but I feel the urgency as if I can already hear the patient's cry for help. I can hear it and feel it and so, like a magnet, I move toward it, as does my partner. We have about fifty metres of plant-room floor to walk across to wake us up into a fully functioning state. I sit at the wheel of the ambulance but feel far from being completely functioning. It is almost 4 am.

The roller door opens up as we get details of the job. My partner, Libby, takes the radio in her hands and repeats the description of the patient's condition over the air.

'Nine-eighty-four responding to Smith Street for the sixteen-year-old female in cardiac arrest.'

Instantly awake.

It is very early morning and mid week, so we fly quietly through the streets. As we drive past all the houses I imagine everyone lying in bed all warm and comfortable. It's so quiet. It's comforting to know that people are safe in their homes, and I'm wondering what on earth has happened in the home we're rushing to. How is it that a young girl is in cardiac arrest?

The street signs reflect our red and blue beacons in a beautiful display of bouncing colour; there's no need for the siren unless we hit a red light. I focus on the quickest route. I know these streets like the back of my hand so it's easy for me, but I still concentrate on getting us to this location as quickly and safely as possible. Since I'm driving tonight it's my job to get us there, assist my partner clinically and mostly keep my mouth shut. After the job, I'll clean up and restock the ambulance and the kits. I'm the wing man and tonight I'm working with one of my best mates, so the teamwork will be really smooth.

We work together. To an outsider it may seem like I take more of a back seat in this partnership, but it's not really the case. I'm absolutely with my partner all the way, I'm just not the dominant voice. Mentally we will be in sync, both of us knowing what to do and how to do it. The driver should be the quiet pillar of support and strength for their partner.

'It's a hanging, Sand, CPR in progress,' Libby says as the gears of the truck drop back and lurch us forward even faster.

In simple terms cardiopulmonary resuscitation is pushing on the chest. Every first-aid course teaches this skill, but even if you have never done it before, as most people haven't, when you call triple zero for assistance the call takers are trained to talk you through the motions of this potentially life-saving manoeuvre. Typically it involves kneeling beside the unconscious patient and pushing firmly on the breastbone around one hundred times a minute. This force on the chest squeezes the heart muscle, which in turn pumps blood to the vital organs and brain. If there is a reversible cause of the cardiac arrest, this pumping will keep the organs oxygenated until we reverse the cause. Time is of the essence, however, and if it has been too long there is no bringing the patient back.

'Righteo, mate,' I say, as I take a deep breath in then out.

'We'll be there in under one minute,' I add in a cool voice. It's really important to get the navigation right; we're working with precious seconds here. Libby has given me all the information I need, and we both know we're walking into a big job. We both know the drug doses, clinical interventions and treatment required. Age is always important and a sixteen year old means adult dosages of medications, so that alleviates a mental burden. Now we are anticipating the emotional trauma and potential difficulties of the scene. It's time to focus, remain calm and connected to each other through these simple points of communication.

'Yep, it's third on the left here, Sand,' Libby says as she pulls the blue latex gloves on and pops the safety glasses on her head.

It's often the way: the bigger the job the calmer and quieter the paramedics, and Libby is already in this zone. The mind needs to be clear on a job like this. We both have enough experience to know we're about to walk into an emotionally charged scene: sometimes the family is screaming; sometimes they scream at us; sometimes they are completely silent, struck dumb from the terror and shock of it all. It's never easy or predictable walking into a hanging.

I bring the ambulance to a halt and we both get out and head to the side door. I wonder to myself if Libby is still stoked to be working overtime with me. Simultaneously, I ponder the unusual fact that paramedics almost always attend the biggest jobs on overtime shifts. *Weird how that happens*, I catch myself thinking for a fleeting second before I'm yanked back to the present.

A young woman is awaiting our arrival out at the front of the premises. Her mouth is slightly open as if part of her has frozen, and she looks as though she's asking herself if this is really happening.

Perhaps she thinks she's in a dream, about to be woken by her alarm clock to get up for work. She doesn't say anything, just walks quickly to the side of the house and opens a gate for us to step through. My heart aches for her already, whoever she is: something terrible has happened to someone she knows.

We're carrying a lot of gear but it feels relatively light, which is another weird thing that happens on the serious jobs. The mind is elsewhere, already with the patient. I'm not concerned with my own physical difficulties or challenges – no mental groan about the weight of the drug kit or having to climb stairs with it. It's just: *get me in there as quickly as possible!* Fuelled by an energy that feels as if it's not my own I feel a pull towards the patient, an urgency to get to her that intensifies with the terror I see on the faces looking on. Perhaps this is one of the differences between a job and a vocation: every bit of me is engaged here, there is such momentum.

Like many people, I have a fantasy image of the perfect, loving home. The kids get tucked into bed with a lingering aroma of the perfect family meal. Maybe there is a log fire that crackles into the wee hours of the morning. Mum and Dad fall asleep in each other's arms talking about how proud they are of their children. The cat curls up on the lounge. The carpet is soft and the porch light is left on for the eldest child, who isn't home yet. It's easy to look at this fantasy and find the love; it's pretty and perfect.

In this ideal fantasy, the teenage daughter keeps a messy room and dreams about innocent romances. In this fantasy there may be tears on the pillow but love prevails, and a mother's hug fixes everything, right? Love makes us hope for the best, and we hope those we love most will know how loved they are. However, we cannot control this and sometimes we are forced to find love in the darkness.

135

As we enter the life of this family through the side gate then on through the garage door, I hear a sound I can't quite figure out. It's vocal, I know that much, almost like a croupy cough. It's rhythmic. Someone is marking time with this sound, barking one constant syllable out through the quiet night air: 'Hrgh, hrgh, hrgh, hrgh, hrgh.' *What on earth is that noise?* I think as we approach the scene.

As we enter the garage we find something more about this morning that smashes my fantasy of domestic love: a man kneeling at the side of a beautiful young girl pushing rhythmically on her chest, counting just under his breath '… thirteen, fourteen, fifteen, sixteen …'.

Every chest compression causes her to make a strange barking sound. The noose has been cut from her neck and the deep-tissue trauma is obvious. *Crushed larynx? Broken neck? Shit, this is not looking good*, I think as my clinical brain kicks in and I analyse the patient's anatomy and physiology.

I know what my partner's thinking and she knows what I'm thinking. We're standing in someone's private hell and we know the outcome is going to be devastating. We position ourselves so we can take over from what must be the most awful experience of this man's life. I will take over the chest compressions and Libby will take care of the airway. This is a familiar set-up now, paramedics going through the motions of a cardiac arrest drill with the family watching and waiting for the news, hoping against hope.

Libby and I exchange a few quiet words and looks between us to confirm we're thinking the same thing. Cardiac arrest as a result of a hanging often means brain death, compounded by the fact the family cannot confirm how long the patient was hanging. It feels futile. I ask the man to move aside so I can take over the work of chest compressions which he does, albeit reluctantly. I press the heel of my left hand hard on the patient's mid-sternum and the heel of my right hand presses on my left. I keep time, pressing rhythmically on her chest while we take these moments to decide how far to go with resuscitation. Every time I press on her chest, air is forced from her lungs and she barks: her final, unintelligible words, filling the dead of night.

We try in vain in these moments to call her back, to change her mind, to plead with her not to do this. Her only response is the raspy bark we force from her. No words, just this god-awful sound we push out of her. She has the full attention of everybody present: two paramedics, two parents, two siblings and a neighbour. We're here pleading with her not to die, but she cannot respond, she cannot speak. If only we could rewind time to the seconds before she tied the noose and grab her by the shoulders and shake her hard, and demand she tell us what's wrong so we can help. But we cannot; she made the decision in the privacy of her own mind.

As I push on her chest, Libby pushes air into her through the bag/mask ventilator. Both of us note her cold hands and fixed, dilated pupils. We read the clinical signs that tell us the story of the moments before our arrival. Once a certain amount of time has passed, even our best efforts cannot call someone back.

'We just need a few details, Dad, can you tell us how you found her?' Libby says to the man who was doing compressions. He is wide-eyed but focused. He has obviously been functioning well in the face of this horror, which is as impressive as it is tragic.

'I just had this feeling to get out of bed, I can't explain it,' he says. 'I went to check on her sleeping, but she wasn't in bed. I walked out here and found her hanging. She used my rope here, how does she know how to tie a bloody noose?' He puts his fingers to his temples, trying to put the pieces together. He seems confused as he recounts events. He looks at his wife, who is standing on the step that leads into the house with her mouth wide open and her hand across it.

'Okay, and then what, you cut her down?' Libby continues, as I push on the patient's chest, counting out loud to prompt the next inhalation cycle.

'Twenty-eight, twenty-nine, thirty,' I say quietly but loud enough for Libby, to prompt her to force a breath into the girl's lungs.

'So we don't know what time she did this?'

'No idea, we'd been asleep since ten,' the father responds. His shoulders drop a little as it becomes obvious to everyone present that the situation is fatal. The cardiac monitor we've placed on her bare chest shows a flat line, indicating her body's absolute lifelessness. Her eyes stare ahead, appearing to be gazing out of the garage into the dark night outside. I see Libby's eyes too, so alert yet soft. In that moment, when our eyes meet, she shakes her head ever so slightly. I respond with a nod and mouth 'yep, okay' to indicate I've registered her decision and that I agree with her.

In less than a minute we've decided that resuscitation is futile, that this patient is beyond our help. I take my hands off her chest, Libby removes the oxygen mask from her face and I cover her bare chest with her clothing. There is a moment of quiet that pierces us all; it's over, she's gone.

'Oh, my God,' says Mum. I look at Libby as she sits there on the floor next to the girl. She places the airway mask on the ground and looks at Mum; there are no words, just a few deep breaths and an exchange of gazes in what is perhaps the longest ten seconds of our lives. The silence brings a little peace, as there was an agony in the patient's last barking sounds that was hard to bear. Now that agony is over, making room for a new, different agony.

Where is the love in this nightmare? A father is not meant to pound on his teenage daughter's chest in a futile attempt to bring her back to life. The garage is not meant to be a place where a girl hangs herself. We are not meant to introduce ourselves after announcing that this family member is dead, and a sixteen year old is not meant to know how to tie a noose. None of this happens in my fantasy of domestic love. It all feels so wrong, and I can see everyone is struggling to make sense of this madness.

I announce on the portable radio that the patient is deceased and the dispatcher takes the cue to call the police. We invite the family into the house for a debrief, a chat ... a something.

I cannot help but fall in love with this family. Throughout the house I notice photos of young people smiling, a family sitting on a green lawn. On a bookshelf there's a picture of a kid sitting on Santa's knee. The house is warm; someone thought of putting the heaters on. The place is clean. I see the name of one of the girls on a bedroom door. To all my senses this is an abode of love.

The family sits together in the lounge room. Mum busies herself in the kitchen.

This is the time when paramedics get to know the characters in a horror movie. First we learn their names, then we get the highlights of the story. Dad tells us there was a recent drama and the school counsellor had been involved. He catches himself saying this, is launched into the present and collapses with grief. This beautiful family is holding hands as if to prevent each other from falling through the cracks in the floor.

As treating officer, Libby is the dominant voice in this debrief. She talks in a heartfelt and compassionate way. One of the many things I love about her is her tact without compromising honesty.

I sense her navigating for the family. There is a tiny light in a pitch-black tunnel, and it is Libby's voice talking about what has just happened and the procedures that now need to take place. She tells them there will be someone here to help them through every step of the process, first us then the police. It is one very little step at a time from here.

And so we make a start on reassembling the millions of scattered pieces; love is being delivered to the family through us right now. Libby's soft but assertive guidance brings Mum and Dad into some sort of functionality, and wide-eyed shock melts just enough that they can support the other kids. Regardless of our roles, we are part of this in a universal way. Suddenly we are all family, bonded in the deep compassion that acknowledges the tragedy, pain and despair the girl must have felt. It is this very tragedy that opens a portal for the influx of love; like a tide it naturally returns, and with it comes newness and a different feeling.

Another woman enters the room with her hands over her mouth and her eyes huge. I assume she is a neighbour or at least a close friend, as she is wearing Ugg boots and purple pyjamas.

'It's Sarah – she hung herself!' Dad says. There are more eruptions of raw grief from everyone in the room. A cool part of my paramedic brain takes note that this is a typical and normal response to an incident like this.

We are all seated around a large coffee table. The sofa is huge and fits everyone. Mum is standing, and Libby is sitting on a hard-backed chair. Mum is strangely cool, but I can tell she is almost completely detached from her grief at this stage. She is a lioness protecting the rest of her pride, not allowing her own vulnerability to emerge; she is fully focused on the others.

Love takes many forms. As I suspend all judgement of what love *should* look like, it starts to appear everywhere. The absence of grief does not mean an absence of love; it means love is so strong that it drives Mum to busy herself with making tea and fussing over people. The neighbour's stupefied reaction doesn't mean she doesn't care; rather, it heralds deep sympathy and compassion for her friends and fear of the pain this will bring. The lifeless form in the garage is stirring all of this love; she is the one connected to each and every one of us and I hope that somehow, somewhere, she feels this love.

Then there are the paramedics. We stand in the middle of the room, in the middle of this scene with all its intensity, trying to find that balance between being professional and being human. We do not know these people and yet here we are on the sofa with them, sharing in the most difficult moment of their lives. Our blue cargo pants and over-shirt with the reflective 'Paramedic' lettering on it are all that differentiate us in this tragedy.

Then Mum looks around and notices that at least three people in the room are wearing purple clothes. 'Look, Anne, your purple pyjamas match the others,' she says in a light-hearted way that breaks some kind of ice in the space. Anne looks like she just got out of bed too, a caring neighbour who dashed over when she saw the ambulance out the front.

In this moment we all smile at each other, acknowledging our daggy humanness, the mundane. For a second there are not only smiles but also laughter at the kooky colour coincidence.

I look at Libby, who has been a silent witness with me for the past ten or so minutes. We smile at each other and I see little dams filling in the bottom of her eyes. Her lower lip quivers a little. 'Don't you start,' I say to her under my breath, feeling a surge of panic at the thought of bursting into tears here myself.

Emotion in the eyes of your partner is like yawning: it's contagious. Suddenly I can feel the gnawing ache in my chest, the tightness in my throat, the heat in my eyes. The natural thing to do in a situation such as this is cry, to express grief at this terrible loss of life. The worst part is the love that perhaps our young patient didn't feel when she took her own life. Could she not feel the love that I see in the eyes of her family? All of this sadness seems to be about that. I imagine she couldn't see it, and that she paid the ultimate price for freedom from her pain and isolation, and I want to double over with my face in my hands and sob. But of course I deny these feelings; I am calm and strong in my role. I pull myself away from the feelings, discretely releasing them on my out-breath.

Libby holds my gaze and offers the slightest gesture of 'Well?' She shakes her head ever so slightly, raises an eyebrow and purses her lips. I read her body language and understand she is saying to me: 'This is so sad, Sand, why can't I cry like them, I'm devastated too.' Instead I look away from her, glancing once again at the parents to see how they're going.

The love in the room is palpable, even if it is covered in grief. At the moment she took her life our young patient must have been in such darkness, and everyone who is left mourns this. All the love in the world couldn't get through to her; it wasn't enough, and grief is the price the family must pay for that love.

There is something about both the family's composure and their vulnerability that makes it impossible for me to avoid my own feelings. Once again I'm reminded that I too am human and, like it or not, I'm now in a relationship with this family. I am involved; I am part of this story now. *It's okay, Sand,* I tell myself. *It's okay to feel this. Let's just not burst into tears though, hey.*

I can't look at Libby, because if I look at her I will certainly lose it and that won't help the family. I stand up and walk over to the kitchen and pour a glass of water. I take the glass to the dad, who is sitting on the couch squeezing his other daughter's hand.

'Here's some water if you need it,' I say to him.

'Oh, yeah, thank you,' he says, and takes the glass.

'You know, the CPR you did was perfect,' I offer. 'You did everything right. She was gone before you cut her down. You do know that, don't you?'

'Yes, the lady on the triple-zero call talked me through it,' he says. 'She was on the phone the whole time. I didn't thank her. I never said anything. She kept telling me to push on her chest, so I did.

'I didn't even hang up the phone,' he adds without shifting his gaze. His thoughts and emotions are clearly jumping all over the place.

'That's fine,' I tell him. 'She would have known when we arrived and she would've hung up. You did everything perfectly. Remember that, okay?'

'Oh my God, oh my God,' he says to himself as he is wracked by fits of uncontrolled sobbing. We all sit still and allow the tears. The sound pierces the stillness of the night, and I'm sure everyone in the street is awake now.

When the police arrive we tell them what has happened and introduce them to the family. It's time for us to retreat, to say our goodbyes and return to the vehicle, to extricate ourselves from this swirling mix of love and loss. To head back to the station through the quiet streets, hoping our loved ones are resting at home peacefully, that the guys back at the station are still fast asleep, that soon the dawn will bring a beautiful day. These are the little reminders that soothe my head and heart.

Back in the safety of our ambulance, we can begin to normalise. The gloves are off and the radio on.

'You know what, Sand?' asks Libby, looking at me.

'What's that, mate?' I say, as I glance in her direction.

'It would have been okay to cry back there, to let them know that we get it, that we know how tragic it is. It would have been okay.'

'Yep, you're right, Lib,' I say. 'With that family, I think it would have been okay. But if I'd started, I don't know if I could've stopped.'

I'm still feeling the constriction in my throat. I feel all choked up and this is what I carry home with me from this job. Holding back these tears hurts my throat. Nobody can see my sadness. I see an image of our patient's neck and the deep, visible, disturbing wounds. Suddenly it is terribly apparent how much suffering she endured.

What dressing does one apply to the invisible wounds? How do they heal? I can wash my uniform and remove my shoes, but the images and unanswered questions remain. To the best of my ability I make a conscious decision to let them go. I breathe them out and dissolve the images until they blur and fade. I send my breath to my throat, I send it love and it softens a little. It brings relief and the mood seems to lift.

'Yeah,' Lib says, completely understanding what I mean. Knowing there is a whole dam of uncried tears in there somewhere. Knowing that even though this is our job, it has a huge impact. Knowing you can't get away unaffected.

There is much more than just dust mites and dog poo travelling around with us after the job and we bring this baggage back to the station, to our homes and to our lives with us every time. This is the emotional stuff that haunts us. It sticks and stays and we cannot wash it off. It becomes our invisible burden.

Both quietly grateful for the tunes on the radio, we take a few minutes just to breathe in and out. Every breath allows our hearts to normalise. The intensity settles, and as I drive the ambulance towards the sunrise a new hope enters our hearts. Sydney wakes to another day, the cafes open and the baristas take their places. The promise of a cuppa is never far from a paramedic's mind, the very simple pleasures that soothe the soul.

'Hey,' Libby says, in a slightly more light-hearted tone.

'Yeah?' I respond on a similar note, eyes darting towards her and a softness creeping onto my face.

'The sun's coming up, do you want to go to Caluzzi's for a cup of tea and Vegemite toast?'

'Oh yeah! That sounds great. I love their sourdough toast. They do a great ginger jam too, you know,' I say as I turn left into Oxford Street and step a little firmly on the accelerator.

'Toast would be nice, yummy!' Libby says, with relief and anticipation.

With enough said for now, it's time to head for a dawn breakfast. Slowly but surely normality seeps back in with the rising sun, and another job fades away with the darkness.

The love between Libby and I has grown too through this shared experience of grief and loss. We will process and file the job in our own way, but the bond we make through this experience is real and strong. It is glued with empathy, strengthened with respect and held through time by love. We will probably shed our uncried tears through raucous laughter around an unrelated topic in the years to come, such is the immense connection and power of love between paramedics. Truly it is a love like no other.

11
WHEN DEATH KNOCKS

Life asked Death, why do people love me but hate you? Death responded,
because you are a beautiful lie and I am a painful truth.
– Unknown

Death never arrives at the right time, a fact that unites us all. Death is like that difficult friend who pops in at great inconvenience when we least expect it. Demanding his dues, he robs us of our beloved and any chance to see, touch and talk to them ever again. Death rudely disrupts our delusion that we have endless time, that love and laughter will go on forever, that we will always have another opportunity to express how we feel. Death has my front door key and he has yours, and he chooses when he enters.

As paramedics we race to people who call us, terrified by this intruder. Sometimes, however, it is too late: Death has been and gone, leaving nothing but a body on the floor.

When it is someone's time to go, it's their time to go and that is that. We paramedics always do our best, and to know that our actions have prevented a death is indeed something special. The flipside is having the humility and self-esteem to accept that our very best is often not enough to bring a person back from the brink. We need to respect the process of dying as being normal and natural; sometimes it feels as though society has forgotten this.

Death so often comes as a terrible and unacceptable shock, even when it is expected. Why do so many of us hold the belief that we are meant to live until our mid-eighties or even older? Anything less is seen as wrong, as being too soon or the person too young. Imagine if we lived each day with no expectation of growing old, that there was no 'normal' time to die. Imagine knowing this very day could be your time to die. Imagine accepting that not all souls want the experience of ageing in a nursing home, wearing nappies at age ninety and eating mush.

Now, imagine having the freedom to celebrate death when it comes, knowing that your soul has completed its work in this body and now gets to go home. Without denying the human experience of grief we can accept that death, no matter when it comes, is somehow perfect for the soul. If we did accept all this, what would we do differently? What words would we free from the heart? Would we be quicker to forgive? Would we be a little more honest, perhaps? One thing is for sure, when that moment comes something happens. With the death of a loved one comes an instant appraisal of our shared life with the departed and of our own lives.

Faced with a thousand forms of fear, our false beliefs come crashing down like a flimsy house of cards, flattened in a second. 'She is strong enough to get through this,' we say, or 'We will beat this thing.' Which leads to the very next thought: 'This cannot be so!' Just before this moment, though, we paramedics usually walk through the door, the last glimmer of hope and the last opportunity for Death to change his mind.

A thirty-eight-year-old woman is in apparent cardiac arrest so we drive like the clappers to get to the scene. With such a young person, we often get a good result with resuscitation. My mind explores possible causes on the way to the scene and there aren't many, given the patient's age – anything under sixty is young to us. First I think trauma, such as a hanging, but there is always the possibility of domestic violence. So many reversible causes to consider: maybe a drug overdose, asthma attack, allergic reaction or choking?

Fate is either on our side or it's not; we all know we're working with precious minutes here. With every thirty seconds, more heart muscle and brain cells die. And the problem with many modern Sydney apartment blocks is that they're like rabbit warrens. At this location there are half a dozen identical blocks all housing multiple units, and we find ourselves driving around searching for the right one. On one level it's incredibly frustrating; on another, it's the universe conspiring in ways that are simply beyond our control.

The rabbit-warren factor runs high on this job. It helps that it's daylight, and my partner and I split up to search for the correct unit number on the doors. Since arriving we have had more information down the data terminal, telling us the patient is palliative. On the back of this information I make immediate assumptions.

'Mate, just so you know, I don't believe in resuscitating the dead. If she is end-stage cancer then we may not even start,' I say to my partner, being open and transparent about my stance on the process of dying.

Over my years as a paramedic, forced resuscitations in absurd situations have become a real issue as people lose their grasp on reality around death. Walking in to find an attendant performing violent chest compressions on a ninety-eight-year-old lady in a nursing home is preposterous, and yet it happens.

Then you have stroke victims, with no quality of life, in adult nappies and being fed through a tube to their stomach. Families either make requests for us to do everything, or an advanced care directive cannot be found or hasn't even been completed and then we arrive. It seems absurd to attempt to maintain life in an organism that is diseased and lifeless, but we live in a world in denial and fear of this process so that everything must be done to prevent death.

Therefore, under great pressure and demand we will pound on a frail chest, knowing it will achieve nothing. We feel every rib crack under our hands. We force the air in and are often met with an eruption of vomit in our faces. Sometimes there will be trauma to the mouth during difficult intubations on bathroom floors. If we cannot cannulate the forearm, we will insert a large-bore cannula into the jugular vein on the side of their neck. Sometimes the elderly heart just won't stop fibrillating, so we deliver shocks of electricity until the smell of burning hair and skin fills the air – often at the family's request, because they believe a few chest compressions mean their loved one simply won't die.

It happens over and over again, and because of this relentless battle with our relationship to death I make my position clear to my partner early on. I really don't want to go in guns blazing, raising expectations. After a few years in the job most paramedics will be on the same page with this one.

'Oh, yeah, I get it,' my partner responds, perhaps a little unsure. As we walk around wasting time looking for the right unit we can only assume the caller is with the patient, probably doing solo CPR guided by the triple-zero call takers, who give incredible guidance and support over the phone. It's a tough gig, I reckon, not being able to see the job in front of you; the call taker's stress may be worse than my own. Hats off to them, I say – they do a remarkable and mostly thankless job.

It takes many years on the job and much exposure to the same thing to gain confidence with decision making; wisdom is gained through trial and error. I recall a job I attended about ten years before this one: distraught over the passing of their chronically ill and elderly loved one, a family member begged us to keep delivering electric shocks. We knew the heart wasn't responding but gave another round to satisfy the family. At that stage we were literally cooking muscle and burning skin, and the smell of burning flesh and singed chest hair took a long time to dissipate. Administering electric shocks to satisfy a grief-stricken yet ill-informed family has led to wisdom: I won't do it any more.

We finally find the unit, having endured maybe six minutes of that nightmare feeling where the scene drags on and on and I want to speed things up but I'm running slowly. You know the feeling? Welcome to 'paramedic brain'; we get that feeling a lot. We're constantly aware of the emergency awaiting our attention but trying to remain calm so we're not flustered when we walk in the door. It certainly is a hard balance to strike.

Up a thousand flights of stairs, as is always the way, and straight in through the front door. A young man, perhaps of Indian descent and wide-eyed and desperate, meets us.

'Oh, thank you, thank you, madam,' he declares. 'You must be quick! You must help us. She is in the bedroom. Please be quick, madam. Please hurry, please hurry.'

'Hello, help is here, show us the way to the patient,' I say as we squeeze our cumbersome equipment through the front door, down the hallway and then through the bedroom door to the patient.

She is on the floor and appears to be dead. She has wet herself, and her clothes reveal her belly and some of her underwear. My immediate instinct is to preserve her dignity and just straighten her clothes but of course I don't do that, I get the facts. In this moment I am faced with one of the biggest decisions a paramedic will face: to attempt resuscitation or not.

'You must help her! She is very sick, madam! She has stage four cancer. GBM, madam,' the young man says rather matter of factly.

GBM is not taught in all the pre-hospital emergency care books. A paramedic's mental database fills up with all sorts of weird and wonderful medical facts depending on what we're exposed to, but I know that GBM is glioblastoma multiforme, a vicious and mostly inoperable brain tumour.

Okay, then, GBM, there is little viability here, I think. I've mentally done the math: up to twenty minutes with ineffective CPR and an aggressive brain cancer. There are no signs of life: the patient is motionless, there is no movement in her chest, no attempts to breathe. Her extremities are a little mottled, which tells me the heart has been stopped long enough to allow a pooling of blood. Her skin is blue in places, especially around the lips, which indicates she has been starved of oxygen for some time, that the cells have sucked the oxygen from the red blood cells with no opportunity to refill in the lungs. I can tell by her colour roughly how long she's been without oxygen. Her body temperature is warm at the core but cool at the extremities. She has been dead for between ten minutes and half an hour. The urinary incontinence means her brain shut down some time ago and that perhaps she had a seizure prior to her death, as this often causes incontinence and can also cause terminal cardiac arrhythmias, where the heart goes into a funny rhythm that cannot sustain blood pressure. There has been a process to her death: death resulting from an aggressive overgrowth of cancerous tissue in the brain. Her time has come.

We're not working, I affirm to myself. The instinct is strong; she is gone.

There are three other paramedics here with me, my partner and another crew. All of us are capable of making this call, however, given my senior clinical rank of intensive care and the fact that we walked in the door first, I take the lead.

'Just pop the leads on, let's see what's going on,' I say to the others. I have already made the gestures to indicate my decision, and when we see no activity on the Lifepak heart monitor we all concur. It's so important to get team consensus and to do so while maintaining absolute respect and dignity for the grieving family.

'Are we all on the same page here, guys?' I ask. 'I am thinking stage four cancer plus downtime means don't start, although I'm open to any other opinions.'

'Yep, I agree.'

'Yes, that's okay with me.'

'Agreed.'

I'm relieved by the responses. At the end of the day, this patient is in the last stage of a terminal illness. Although her colour is quite good and we would almost certainly have a positive effect on her otherwise well heart, I know this is the right thing to do for her.

'What are you doing? Use your machine, you have to help her!' the young man shouts at us, almost hysterical.

'What's your name, sir?' I ask.

'Ranjeep is my name, madam. But you are wasting time with these stupid questions! Please, you must help her!'

'And what is your relationship to this woman, Ranjeep?'

'She is my wife! Oh my god, oh my god, oh my god! Sakeem, my love, my love, you cannot do this to us! I am not ready! No, no, no, no! Please!' he screams at us and his beloved. He falls onto his knees by her side, yelling her name at her lifeless body.

My eyes dart to the other paramedics, and we allow the process. I watch Ranjeep's actions, mindful that I won't allow any aggression towards her even though she is dead. I am still mindful of preserving her dignity and making this moment as peaceful as possible. On one level she is still here; I sense her presence in the room and I want her to have peace and quiet as she transitions out of her sick body. In a perfect world there would be candles and soft music, there would be a calm, peaceful and sacred space to assist the spirit to leave the body and return to its source. There would be love and support but no attachment, there would be a space of great allowing and quiet celebration for this moment of departure.

'Ranjeep, would you like to step out of the room for just a moment with me while we remove the equipment from her?' I say as warmly as possible. The strategy here is to calm him down and assist him to assimilate this information, as clearly he is not mentally prepared for this moment.

'Madam, nobody is leaving this room! You can save her! Why are you not trying? All of that machinery, the electricity, why are you not doing something? I call you for help. I am not ready to let her go, not ready. This is too soon! One more minute, that is all I ask, bring her back for one more minute. I must speak with her. I do not know how to do life without her. Please, you must, really. Please now, you do whatever you can do.'

'I am so sorry for your loss. She's dead, Ranjeep, there's nothing we can do to bring her back. I am sorry. I understand she was very sick with advanced cancer of the brain. Did the doctors tell you she was going to die?'

'Yes, they tell me all the time! But I have researched, I know all the answers! I have been fixing her cancer, I have put her under this special light, see?' He indicates an elaborate lighting system by the bed with what appear to be ultra-violet bulbs.

'Yes, I can see that. You have done everything you could have done,' I say, acknowledging this elaborate system of fancy lights positioned at the head.

'You must do something, please!' he pleads desperately again. We stand there steadfastly, offering eye contact and simple gestures of support. Thankfully the phone in his hand rings, and he answers the call then bursts into tears, running into the lounge room and speaking in another language.

With a few moments to ourselves we can have a chat to each other about the situation. We are all too familiar with this process, but it never makes it any easier. For many paramedics it is awkward and difficult, as we don't always have the answers people want. Loved ones often don't understand the basis for our decisions, and it can take time to win their trust. Emotions are running high and words don't seem to make sense.

'Is everybody happy with this decision?' I check in with the team.

'Yes, Sand, absolutely. Should we put her back in the bed?'

'Yeah, I think that's a good idea. Let's just ask him though, make sure it's okay to move her. Has someone called the cops?'

'Yep, they're on their way, all good. We can stick around as long as you need us.'

'Yes, great, thanks for that. If you can stick around until he settles

155

down a bit and we put her back to bed, that would be great. Then you can clear.'

'Okay, no drama.'

Ranjeep interrupts our conversation as he charges back into the bedroom in full-blown tears.

'What are you doing? Why do you do nothing? Just bring her back for some minutes. Five minutes, that is all I ask. Please, you can do that. It is not time, not now. One more minute, please. Come now, you must. It is your job, yes?'

'Ranjeep, no. We cannot do that. Her time has come, she has died.'

'She has not died! I am not believing you!' he sobs, then returns to her lifeless body. He cries aloud, holding her face in his hands. We stand there, keeping a space for his process and making no attempt to stop him crying. A rapid process is unfolding here: all Ranjeep's delusions are crashing down around him. He believed in a miraculous remission of illness with no thought of death, and I see his tears, hysteria and denials as necessary and normal.

'It's not your fault, Ranjeep, you did everything you could. It is her time,' I offer, hoping these words will assist him to come to some acceptance of the situation.

'For months I have been fixing her! I understand the laws of nature, it is possible to beat this thing! I have research, I know what to do! There is no reason the cancer should be killing her. I have given her juices, the special lamp light every night, we will beat this thing!'

'I hear that, Ranjeep, and I can see how much you have done: it's amazing. I can see how much you love her. You have done so much, but sometimes even that is not enough.'

'This is bullshit!' he yells, as he storms out of the bedroom. The phone rings a second time; relatives in India, I assume. He screams into the phone and bursts into tears again. We follow him into the lounge room and I take a seat on the couch. It doesn't seem to be helping, speaking over the body of his wife.

My partner is in the kitchen and the other crew is waiting outside to meet the police and bring them in. This can take up to an hour or more, and I can only assume they're giving us some space to have this discussion. Sometimes it is a team effort, the talking, and sometimes it is not. I think we would all agree, that given Ranjeep's lack of acceptance and emotional hysteria this is a tough gig, but we continue. He ends his call and runs back into the bedroom. I choose not to follow but to give him time in there alone with his wife. Within a minute he is back in the lounge room with me.

'I have a son, he is ten years old. For the last six months I tell him every day, "Your daddy will fix this, Mummy will be fine. Everything will be fine. Mummy is getting better every day." We stay at home because I refuse to go to the place of dying.'

'Okay, I hear that, Ranjeep. Has there been any discussion about death at all?'

'No! The doctors tell me the whole time that she will die but I refuse to believe it. I believe in the laws of nature, that this can be fixed!' he says, in a slightly lower volume than before. He pauses, looks around and offers a slight smile to my partner, as if he has seen him for the first time. He glances to a seat at a table that holds mountains of tablets and he sits down. He looks at the medication, then at the notes he has been making in a diary next to them. He is slowing down, and it looks as though he is taking it all in now; he is still wide-eyed, but a little more relaxed. As he relaxes, I relax.

Moments ago the scene did not feel completely safe, with his volatile outbursts, but now it feels like somehow we are all friends here.

'Okay, yes, I can see that. I really hear that you believe you can fix this. I see how much you love your wife. She is a very lucky woman,' I say with a warm smile.

'Oh no, madam, she gets very upset with me for doing this. I am a very painful husband for her!' he says, and he smiles cheekily at me, shaking his head.

Finally! He's responding, thank you God, I think as I let out a long, inward sigh.

'There is a lot of love in your marriage,' I respond in a calm, soft voice.

'Yes, too much love, madam, too much love,' he says before pausing a few moments.

'Ranjeep, do you have any spiritual beliefs?'

'I believe in nature. I am not Hindu, like my wife, I have no religious beliefs.'

'Okay. Can I ask you a question?'

'Yes, madam.'

'If we think of nature, all the creatures and all the countries, the weather patterns, the ocean, the volcanoes ...'

'Yes, madam.'

'Sometimes, the most beautiful places are destroyed by natural disasters. And baby animals die young. Sometimes they die from other animals, or injury and disease.'

'It is true, madam. It is true, I do not doubt this.'

'Then is it possible to see ourselves as part of this? We are part of nature, too. When Mother Nature says it is time to die, it is time. Shouldn't we have respect for this, respect that Mother Nature is more powerful than us? We cannot prevent a tsunami or a volcano. When Mother Nature says it is time for Sakeem to die, we need to respect this. It is not your fault, Ranjeep. Mother Nature decides when we die, not us.'

For a moment we hold eye contact, and I can see that something has dropped. He's been blaming himself.

'It's not your fault, Ranjeep.'

He sobs into his hands again but he remains in the lounge room, which brings me great relief.

'She is the one who knows how to do all the emotional things!' he says. 'I have no idea. How do I do this? I do not know what to do.'

'Ranjeep, nobody knows how to do it. I think we are all a bit similar this way; I don't know that anyone has all the answers. It's not easy, but you're doing it right now. We are all just doing our best.'

'I tell my wife, you do this emotions stuff, I am not doing so! And she gets very upset with me. But I am the better cook. I never tell this to her. She does not know that I am the better cook.' He throws his head back and laughs out loud, as do I.

'Ah, you are a wise man indeed, Ranjeep,' I say with a wide smile.

I glance towards my partner, who is still standing in the kitchen looking in. He smiles, raises his eyebrows and gives a little nod. We've reached Ranjeep.

Ranjeep is making more eye contact. His pacing has slowed, and I feel like we can start talking more normally now. The intensity in the air has settled as acceptance of Sakeem's death begins to settle. I know we don't have long before the police will come. When they get here it will be appropriate for us to leave, so any remaining guidance or support really needs to happen now.

With Ranjeep more in control of himself and the situation, I am starting to feel our work here is done. The phone rings again, and Ranjeep takes the call. He is speaking fast this time rather than screaming and standing still as he talks, which is a good sign. My other colleagues enter the room and we take another opportunity to talk.

'Should we put the body back in the bed?' my partner asks.

'Yes, I think so. Let's just ask if it's okay.'

I lean over and ask Ranjeep if he would like this and he replies: 'Yes, madam, please do this.'

Sakeem is no bigger than me but the words 'dead weight' pop into my mind. The four of us reach for a limb each and take great care to hold her head as we lift her back into her bed. We place the blankets neatly around her, straighten her hair and make the bed around her. She looks as if she is sleeping peacefully. With the few seconds I have with her I offer her a silent prayer. I call on her spiritual guides to assist her to transition to where she needs to be. It feels right, and I am relieved she has no broken ribs from futile chest compressions or any other trauma to her body. She appears to be at peace.

As we make our way back out to the lounge room I start thinking of an exit strategy. The other crew is about to leave as Ranjeep ends his conversation on the phone. I am sitting on the couch again and about to wind things up when Ranjeep looks straight at me.

'Madam, I have one question.'

'Yes, Ranjeep, anything at all,' I say, happy that his volume has dropped back down and he appears more engaged.

'How do I tell my son?'

Wow, I think to myself as I draw a slow breath into my chest and take an eternity to breathe out. Our eye contact is not broken, but I can feel my colleagues' gaze upon me. Ranjeep's eyes are sincere, pleading for answers. Suddenly I can see his life laid out in front of him: mid-thirties, single father of a young boy, no friends in Australia and no wife to handle those difficult conversations.

How do you tell a ten-year-old boy his mother has died? There has been no mental preparation. Dad's been playing God and promising to fix her. What the hell do I say?

Of course there is no correct answer, but I can't leave him hanging. I have to give him something.

'Madam, what would you say if it were your very own son, please?'

'I'd tell him the truth,' I say, and sit in a silence that penetrates all parts of me. My words echo out into the universe: it feels like such a risk.

'I'd tell him I did my very best but she died today because today was the day that was her time to die, that just like all the creatures of the world have their time this is hers. I'd tell him it's nobody's fault, that sometimes even our very best effort is not enough to prevent someone dying if it is the right time for them to die, that his mother's death may not feel like the right time to him but it was the right time for her. I'd tell him I love him very much and will do my very best with him too. I'd tell him I may not have all the answers but I have all the love in the world, and the love we feel for Mum will keep her in our hearts forever.'

'Okay, madam, my wife is liking this, I think. And will you be waiting here with me for my son to be home from school? This is best I think, madam. He is a good boy. Very good at soccer, too.'

'Oh, Ranjeep, I would have loved to meet your son. He is a very lucky boy indeed, he has the best father in the whole world! And I just know that whatever words you choose to say to him will be perfect too. I am not saying it will be easy, I am just saying that your love and your heart are enough. Your words will be perfect for him.'

'Oh, I do not think so, madam. You must pray, madam! Please, pray for my son. That he is okay without his mother. Please. Will you do that?'

'Absolutely,' I promise, surprised by his request but sure I will commit to this and satisfied that our work here is finally done. In perfect timing, too, as we hear a knock at the door and both know it is time. I stand and extend my hand to his.

'I'm sorry for your loss, Ranjeep, the police will help you now. It's our time to leave. Please take care. I promise to pray for you, your wife and your son.'

As I walk down the stairs away from the scene, I take a long, full breath in and exhale completely. I let all the heaviness and stress of that conversation leave my body through my breath. Whatever bond formed between me and this lovely family has been cut. I am very conscious about how I end each job. It is done, and all parts of my spirit leave the scene with me; I leave nothing behind. It's my personal way of ensuring I'm not drained.

Precious time after jobs like this one gives me a much-needed opportunity to get myself back together. Not just physically, but emotionally and energetically. After washing my hands and a short debrief with my partner, I take a moment in quiet meditation to clear me of any negativity or heaviness. As my partner cleans various items, I sit in the sun with my eyes closed and breathe in from way above my head.

I use this time to take a mental shower. Brilliant electric violet light pours through me as I will it with a powerful intention. I imagine little taps on my hands and feet can open up as this waterfall of light washes through me, pouring out of my extremities. My breath guides this light, my inhale drawing clean light in from above me and the exhale releasing the heaviness, grief and sickness. It takes only a few minutes of breathing in this way until the cleansing light that flows from my hands and feet becomes clean and bright. The sun feels gorgeous, I feel lighter and my mind rests in the peaceful place of acceptance. I open my eyes in gratitude for my own life and healthy, vibrant body. With this process complete I feel ready for the next case, which thankfully doesn't come until we have picked up a coffee. Then this, like most other jobs, dissolves into nothing.

In the quiet of my own space after my shift and out of uniform, I light a candle for Ranjeep and his family. I say a prayer as requested for his son and in so doing I am flooded with golden light. My heart swells and I can almost hear Sakeem's words of gratitude. The love between these souls seems to fill my body and flood through me. I send this pure, positive energy to Ranjeep and his family, and I'm uplifted as I do so. I smile gently at the hope of Ranjeep receiving this energy, and I remind myself that his display of grief only demonstrates the potency of his love for his wife. I rest in the thought that Ranjeep and his son will be okay, that grief, as disturbing as it may feel, is a normal and healthy part of a healing process.

I lay it all to rest, having bathed in the very love I sent them, the same love that washes me tonight, the perfect way to end the day. My sense of gratitude is heightened in the awareness that my door, like all doors, remains open to death and yet death is not here for me tonight. I have time, and the quiet voice of awe whispers to me that *life is so precious, milk every drop, waste nothing*. My pillow feels delicious, my bed so soft. Content and free, I drift off to sleep.

12

SHELTER FROM THE STORM

Love is an element which though physically unseen is as real as air
or water. It is an acting, living, moving force, it moves in waves and
currents like those of the ocean. – Prentice Mulford

I have never set out on a specific search for a spiritual life. By the time I was twenty-five I had notched up five years as a paramedic, I had nearly drunk myself to death, I felt old before my years and was burnt out. I heard somewhere that religion is for people who are scared to go to hell, and spirituality is for people who have already been there. I place myself in the second camp. I had been living with night terrors for years and six of my friends had committed suicide when I stumbled, quite by accident, onto the spiritual path.

I did not go looking for a spiritual teacher, but through my own personal crisis I became ready for one. I never consciously sought love, but it found me. I never asked for help, and yet it was there when I most needed it. These are the manifestations of what I call grace: being blessed through no merit of my own, protected and carried through the storms of life and finding a fulfilment and satisfaction at the deepest level of my being.

My spiritual teacher tells me always to trust, that there are no mistakes with timing and that the divine can see further than I can. I met this wonderful woman at precisely the right time, and although my circumstances then definitely warranted spiritual guidance, really this was just preparatory. There were storms brewing on the horizon of my soul's evolution that I didn't see coming but of which the divine was aware, and so the help came early in the form of this incredible teacher to prepare me for what lay ahead.

We weather many storms, some physical but mostly emotional and spiritual. The 'dark night of the soul' can make us feel like there is no light left for us and the bleakness will never end. A form of initiation, we enter into a process that ends up building the very framework of courage and strength we need for our ongoing journey.

Then there is the tsunami of life that floods in with a seemingly uncanny and cruel timing, such as when your partner leaves you the same day you lose your job and you crash your car on the way home, only to realise your house has burnt down while you were away. You feel as though your life has been utterly devastated.

I was fifteen years into the job when, as fate would have it, I was enjoying three weeks of hard-earned annual leave away from work as a paramedic. For the first time in many years I had not scooted off overseas to climb a mountain, dive the seas or sip on masala chai on the back roads of India. At this time, the Philippines was struck by one of the worst typhoons to date: Typhoon Haiyan, known as Yolanda to the local people. Thousands of people lost their lives and many more were injured and without shelter.

Scrolling through my social media news feed, I noticed an advertisement calling for interested paramedics to deploy immediately for the disaster-stricken Philippines. The timing seemed so perfect. The fact that the owner of the disaster relief company asking for volunteers was a long-term colleague of mine only enthused me even more. Immediately I was drawn in, running through the timing in my mind. I had no commitments for three weeks, I had the perfect skill set and I was super keen for the experience. With no hesitation whatsoever, I applied for the position and advertised myself as being available to deploy immediately.

My well-intentioned self-care annual leave swiftly turned into the adventure of a lifetime, working within a small team of medical and paramedical professionals in a disaster zone. I have many stories from this time, but let me set the scene with just one here.

This is a story about the grace of having a realised spiritual master in my life, and knowing that sometimes help comes to us when it is really needed. I certainly didn't need to be in my teacher's physical presence for this to occur – thank God, because I know for a fact my teacher would have no interest in going to half the places I find myself in!

Let me take you there. It's monsoon time in a remote village about an hour's drive from Tacloban, some 600 kilometres south-east of Manila, the city that took the brunt of Haiyan. It is a few days since the typhoon hit and the entire place is a mess. Those in our team of ten have never met each other before this deployment and we comprise two doctors, two army nurses, two paramedics and four hospital-trained nurses. There are three women in the group: me and two other nurses.

Like many of my colleagues, for years I had wanted to stretch my skills through medical aid work, work that appeared so exciting and would develop me professionally. The only problem is that work commitments on home soil make it nearly impossible for overseas deployment, unless you are attached specifically to a unit that responds to such incidents as directed by the Australian government. So imagine the excitement I feel when I'm invited to join this select team of medicos and travel straight to the disaster zone. The timing – that I have scheduled holidays at this moment – means I'm commitment free and good to go!

With minimal time to plan, let alone pack, I find myself at the team briefing in Cebu, an island west of Tacloban, in a matter of hours. We have time to meet each other and briefly discuss our areas of specialisation and what we each bring to the team. I'm impressed with this group; there is a broad scope of experience and, most importantly, the personalities all fit well together. The days we will spend together will be in close quarters in unpredictable and potentially dangerous conditions.

We carry with us field packs and as much equipment as possible. We're anticipating minor trauma, wounds, medical conditions and infection given that our first contact will be more than a week after the initial typhoon. We know many lives have been lost already, but what we don't know is that the death toll will climb to more than 15,000 people.

Again, as fate or grace would have it, our team manages to organise access into the disaster zone ahead of other major government agencies that had been experiencing delays due to bureaucratic red tape. The moment we hear word that the Royal Australian Air Force can deliver us on the ground we go.

The thundering C-130 Hercules aircraft we travel on has no windows, so we can't see the devastation until we touch down. We've had ear buds handed to us by the army crew prior to take off, so conversation is limited. The heavy vibrations of the engines send the others off to sleep but I'm wide awake, taking in every moment of this adventure and making mental notes of what I need to remember in the event of emergency.

Keep your passport with you at all times, but conceal it. It's worth a lot and we don't want to get taken for ransom. Keep the phone number of our emergency contact with you at all times then, if some drama happens, make your way back to the airfield. If one of our team goes down, use a satellite phone and arrange a medevac [medical evacuation]. No one walks around alone at any time, keep an eye on everybody in the team; don't let them forget this.

'Want some chewy, Macken?' says Barry, the army medic and team leader. He yells into my ear probably a little louder than he needs to, jolting me out of my mental check list.

'Yes, please,' I say, and hold out my hand as Barry pulls the chewing gum out of his mouth in a long strand of minty goo.

'Just kidding,' he says as he puts the gum back in his mouth then reaches into his pocket for a fresh piece. I enjoy the friendly banter; already this group feels like easy company. We've had a few days together by now, planning and discussing tactics and potential dangers and how to meet them, including personal survival tips and medical capability and capacity.

The chewing gum helps me pop my ears as we descend swiftly onto the runway at Tacloban airport, which has been blown apart by Haiyan. It has no roof and is surrounded by mounds of debris, with the runway being the only part that is intact. With engines still fired up and propellers still spinning, we are hurried off the aircraft out the rear then down a ramp that lowers onto the tarmac. No sooner have we rushed over to the side of the runway than the Hercules C-130 takes off under full thrust and disappears into the thick monsoonal clouds.

The destruction is incomprehensible. There are thousands of coconut trees standing like match sticks over the hills beyond the airport and not one has any foliage left. Cars and trucks tipped on their roofs are scattered everywhere, and off in the distance I can see a container ship completely out of the water, listing slightly to one side on what appears to be a road. It's absolute carnage.

'Come, we move you north from here, there is a small village and they have not had medical help yet. There are hundreds of people needing your medical attention,' says our local contact.

We have plans to move out to a more remote area, to access these people. At this stage, there are no international medical aid services on the ground. We had been told that the army had been through in the first few days, which becomes evident when we start to see patients with huge lacerations that the army sutured where possible. For now there is no evidence of any medical assistance.

We make it to our first camp, a small village where some large stone churches are still intact and some cement homes are still standing, but otherwise there are huge piles of debris that were once the rudimentary shanty town which has been completely destroyed. The roads have been cleared so we can drive through, and to either side of the road are piles of timber, houses with no roofs, upside down vehicles and huge piles of rubbish. There is debris in the electrical wires, and by some stroke of fortune we miss the body of the woman who is entangled in these wires more than ten metres in the air. There are bodies all over the place. They float up on the high tide and reveal their location in the days that follow by the foul stench they exude in the heat of the monsoon sun.

Our first clinic is set up in a school. It is a large open room, and we divide it into sections. My section is up the back, where I create a wound clinic and ready myself to see what will be about fifty of the total three hundred patients per day. The first few days in the clinic go really well; we establish a routine and slowly but surely move through the line of people waiting to see us, which at first extends out of the clinic and all the way down the street.

By the third day a little fatigue creeps in. We are sleeping on a wooden floor with a yoga mat for a mattress and a sleeping bag liner as a sheet. No pillows, of course, and no showers, and we three women are sharing a small single room. The mozzies are the size of drones and my neck is playing up; I know I'm moments off a spasm and my clothes are dirty and smelly.

Around day ten we have another drop in general morale, mostly due to the tummy issues with which we are all now suffering. The locals have been kind enough to cook for us, presenting white rice and baitfish pan fried whole. We dare not complain as we know that food and water are extremely limited; it's a blessing we have anything other than our stash of protein balls.

The sun is out and it feels as though we're in a Bikram yoga studio at full capacity. Never been to Bikram yoga? Well, it's hot and humid. Steam is rising off every surface and we're almost drowning in our own sweat. The clean-up has begun and people are burning debris. There are piles of rubbish, a lot of wet wood. The awful thing is there are bodies still buried beneath the mounds of debris and they smell. It's bad. The toxic odour of burning plastic wafts through our clinic, and today is beyond a struggle.

I now have gastro, which doesn't help. For days my role in the clinic has become 'wound gal'. I thought I'd be suturing up lacerations, but it turns out I'm debriding open wounds that never healed closed. Imagine having a deep, open cut through the skin, and instead of closing, the wound starts to dry up in that gaping open position. The body is so intelligent; it will go about its business of healing from the base of the wound up. What happens, though, in the absence of the skin is that the body produces a layer of thick hard slime as the skin attempts to grow underneath. It is sort of like a scab but is softer. This 'biofilm' is a bacteria embedded in a thick slimy barrier of essentially sugars and proteins. Apparent in most chronic wounds, its presence delays healing. In order to maximise the chance of timely healing, this thick biofilm sometimes needs to be removed. By definition, debridement is the removal of non-viable tissue and foreign matter. Although it is not pleasant, when attended to with patience it is a relatively painless procedure.

Unfortunately, some of these wounds stink to high heaven. Along with the offensive smells, there are diabetic toes that appear gangrenous and ready to drop off, open and infected wounds, fungal feet and the ever-present stench of iodine. It is the sort of work environment where fresh lavender would be shoved up the nostrils if it were handy. The toilet is a little mosquito-breeding zone with no ventilation, and the flush system is a bucket of water you fling down after every visit. The mozzie coil fills the tiny room with noxious smoke and the gastro factor doesn't help.

As much as I try to ignore it, the stench wafting into the clinic from the burn-off outside becomes so disturbing I request they desist.

'What the hell are they burning out there?' I call out from my clinic post. I'm sure I'm scowling, and I am feeling pretty pissed off too. I'm outraged at the inconsideration of whoever started the fire right outside the clinic. They're burning something toxic for sure, maybe plastic, but there is a distinct smell of death and there are no windows anywhere to block the smoke. Not knowing the local politics, I have no idea if they are burning the dead but my imagination needs no fodder; it is awful. My greatest sense is smell, which at times like this feels like a great curse!

I sit for a few minutes between patients. I remove my gloves, down a super sweet, strong coffee and sweat it out. I take a moment to look at our little clinic and the long line of locals waiting patiently to be seen. I breathe deeply to alleviate the waves of nausea that threaten to overcome me. All I want right now is to go across the street to our little home and lie down on my yoga mat, but our rotations are all timed and it's not my turn for a rest. Everyone is struggling by this stage, so I dare not indulge in a break while everyone is working. The only respite I get is when I sit in the tiny cement toilet room that is dimly lit by a candle. It stinks in there too, of course, but the mosquito coils overwhelm the senses enough to cover the smell and it's private, like a little holiday from this hell hole of trauma, grief and sadness.

There is an old man waiting to see me when I return from my toilet break. He is large and physically strong, but like so many others looks completely deflated. His shoulders are rounded and his eyes are sad. His hands are resting in his lap, and the two doctors and my nurse roommate are standing around him. I walk over to see if he might be my next wound to clean and immediately see that his injuries are far beyond my scope of practice.

'Okay, just try to open and close your hands, sir,' says Doctor Anthony. I can see his tendons are damaged, deep lacerations running across all his fingers. He can move his thumbs but not his fingers. The lacerations are open and have already begun to heal that way. His fingers are very swollen.

Our translator passes on the doctor's requests for him to attempt to move various fingers in various directions, all to no avail. His hands are going to need surgery, but I don't know if we've got him in time to save his hands and restore movement. The doctors start talking about organising a medevac for this man, and the translator starts to talk to him again. I don't understand what he is saying, but the patient shakes his head in response.

'This man is the grandfather of two small children,' the translator tells us, before looking back to the patient and encouraging him to continue talking. He does so, using minimal gestures and speaking in a low voice.

'This man lives in the village. He says the typhoon hit and the winds were so strong. It was dawn when the storm came. It was the sound of screaming,' he continues.

We are all standing listening to yet another story of trauma and most probably loss. It seems every person who enters the clinic has family and friends who are missing or dead. We all fear the worst from this recounting of events. To be a listening ear has at times been all we can offer, and while this feels frustrating it has hopefully helped unburden the load for some, to know that at the very least we care about their loss. So we listen here again, patiently and with as much compassion as we can.

'After the wind came a tidal surge. He says it was a wall of water, it lifted everything up and carried many things away. This man cannot swim, and neither can his grandchildren. Everything they owned was carried away, as the waters rose and rose,' the translator relays back to us as the patient keeps talking.

'The water rose all the way up to the electrical wires, above the rooftops. The children were getting swept away. They are young, only five and six years old.

'This man grabbed hold of the two children. He held them so tight for so long. The water was trying to rip the children from his grip, but he doesn't let them go. He is floating in the water surge, and he holds the electrical wire with his hands. He is very scared that the children will be ripped from him. He holds so tight, his hands lock, like a cramp, you know?'

'Yes, yes, we understand, go on,' says Doctor Anthony.

'He changes his grip, both hands, see?' the translator says as he points to the deep lacerations that stretch across the man's fingers and palms.

'So, you see, he holds the children with one arm, and with the other hand he holds himself to the electrical wire as the water continues to flood so fast. The whole time this man expecting the children to be ripped from his hands, so he holds on so tight. He feels his hands rip but still he never lets go.'

We are all thinking the same thing, we are imagining those children breaking free from his clutch and drowning like the thousands of others. I think to myself, *His depressed demeanour is so warranted. My God, he just lost his grandkids.*

'We are so sorry this happened to you,' offers one of the nurses. I am glad she spoke, as I know I would have broken down if I had to talk at that moment. The patient is quiet as he gazes into the air. I imagine he is being flooded with those images of which he just spoke. We are all wondering about the children, but nobody dares ask him. The silence is long and heavy, broken only by the translator, who continues to talk at length with the man. He nods as the man speaks back to him, then looks at his hands and shrugs his shoulders.

'He wants you to know that to him, losing the use of his hands is a small price to pay for the life of those children.'

175

'They survived?' I interject immediately.

'Yes, they survived. He said he would have held on until his arms fell off if he had to.'

'Oh, thank God,' I say. We all let out a huge sigh of relief and I'm again flooded with the feeling of wanting to cry. I hold the tears, and we all celebrate the man's heroic efforts with applause and pats on the back. He smiles and nods his head, which feels like such relief.

He has lost the use of his hands, for now anyway, but at least he saved the children! It feels like a win, yet despite this win the emotions stirring within me make me feel nauseated.

The room is spinning and the sense of relief that comes with this latest story seems to open the floodgates in me. I'm saturated with the stench of iodine and open wounds. I have countless images of open wounds and sad faces flooding my being, but it's the smell that is almost killing me. My bowels start churning and for a moment I'm not sure if I'm going to cry, spew or crap myself, so I take a seat and breathe long deep breaths as the sweat pours off me.

Suddenly out of the blue the scent of wild rose fills my senses. I *know* this smell. The first time I was in the physical presence of a living saint I smelled this fragrance, and I have smelled it in the temple with my teacher many times. This is a mystical phenomenon that occurs when the divine is present.

My entire being is transformed: the nausea is gone, I am in complete bliss. The fragrance is the most splendid, intoxicating, delicious gift ever. Instantly I'm aware she is here, as though she has walked into the clinic. And of course she *is* here, through my connection to her. She is here because I am here. I breathe in the fragrance like a drowning person breathes for air. It fills me completely and reminds me I am not alone, that this work is filled with grace, that I'm guided and supported and that spiritual connection is everywhere I am. My heart bursts open as I experience this extraordinary grace. The room is filled with the most delicious blend of wild rose, jasmine and sweetness. The timing could not be more perfect, coming at my lowest point when I am so out of sorts I don't even think to ask for it.

This gift of divine fragrance lifts my spirit in such an incredible way that in an instant all the pain and sadness are gone. The awful images are gone, the feelings of hopelessness are gone, and I am left knowing that everything is going to be all right. Just like that, from a fragrance wafting in out of nowhere.

This connection to grace is one I have through a gift of my teacher. It is ever present, all knowing and precise in method, timing and perfection. That moment when the roses filled my senses gave me the fuel I needed to continue for another few weeks, to assist hundreds of people in their time of need. It was also the shelter from the storm I needed.

This undeniable direct encounter with an internal spiritual support blows my mind for a few reasons. To be rescued by a fragrance is so perfect for me, it's like the divine was making the point that it knows and understands my uniqueness. It feels like such a personal moment even though fragrance is so impersonal, because that specific fragrance is the single most glorious smell I have ever encountered. Not only did it fill my senses, but it also altered my emotions, my energy levels and my spirit all at once.

I went in to this disaster wanting to help others and indeed we did that. What was returned to me was a gift money cannot buy: I was touched by countless hearts who showed me in so many ways just what love looks like. Despite the thousands of deaths and casualties after the typhoon, not one person complained. Despite the lack of equipment and resources to correct many problems effectively, the only words we heard consistently every day were 'thank you'. Despite the trauma and tragedy, we saw communities gather and friendships form. Despite the loss, we saw laughter and kindness everywhere. Despite how Mother Nature seemed to turn on them ferociously and take so many lives, we saw time and time again the enduring human spirit.

We saw hope and gratitude in countless people. We witnessed the rebuilding of faith and the remarkable resilience of the human heart. We saw the global family step in to assist those in need. If there was any shred of burn-out or cynicism in my own heart from years of repeated exposure to death and tragedy, it was healed by the people I had contact with in the Philippines. They restored my own heart, which had weathered many of its own storms. This gift has only grown and expanded in the years since. On some level that mission saved me, in ways I am still appreciating. To be of service to another, no matter how big or small the act of service, has the capacity to activate an unseen power within.

The power of the heart has many flavours and many names. At the end of the day, it is the heart that has the power to lift us and to change us for the better. It is through the heart that we tap into the power of the universe and come to realise that nothing matters much except for love.

ABOUT THE AUTHOR

Sandy Macken is a writer, paramedic and spiritual teacher. She has decades of experience in frontline emergency health, and brings a calm, grounded approach to all she does.

As the bright lights and blazing siren of an ambulance flash by, have you ever wondered what's happened? In *Paramedic: One woman's 20 years on the front line*, her first book, Sandy takes us into the high-pressure world of a paramedic. It's an up-close-and-personal account of racing at high speed to all kinds of emergencies: from a car smash to an overdose, a drowning, a long fall and even suicide. We experience the extraordinary skill and split-second decision making that go into saving lives.

Sandy describes clinical procedures with a no-nonsense precision, but she offers much more than medical knowledge: to each patient she brings compassion, kindness and a rare intuition, and from each trauma she teases out a deeper meaning of love in the face of pain and loss. We also learn about the bonds our paramedics form with one another, and the toll their stressful work can take on their lives. Sandy is not just about helping, she's also about healing – for the body, of course, but also for the heart and soul.

Every one of the stories in the book is a true story, although all personal and place names have been changed to protect identities and privacy.

Sandy holds degrees in health sciences and education and is currently studying a Master's qualification in counselling and psychotherapy. She has extensive professional and personal experience with trauma, deep transformation, building resilience and fostering a blazing spirit.

An energetic and engaging thinker who unites spirituality and practical living, Sandy's blogs have attracted considerable attention and inspired her to write this book. She has also been published in the international medical journal *EMS World*.

High-spirited yet also deeply pragmatic, Sandy is dedicated to fostering good health on all levels, especially among health and helping professionals. 'Peace in the fast lane', Sandy's online hub for inspiration and holistic health tools, also offers face-to-face learning zones to enhance and ignite the spirit.

Sandy lives in Sydney with her partner, and they are looking forward to welcoming their first child in 2018. When she is not working, writing or studying you will find Sandy speaking to groups, teaching meditation or jetting off to India, where her own spiritual teacher lives, to fill up on the healing energy she so readily shares with everyone she meets.

A NOTE TO READERS

The content of this book may be unsettling to some. If you encounter any level of disturbance as a result of reading these stories, please reach out for help. Here are some numbers to call in Australia should you find yourself in need of information or support.

Alcoholics Anonymous is a non-profit organisation providing information and support to anybody seeking help with a drinking problem.

Phone: 1300 222 222

Lifeline is an Australian national charity providing all Australians experiencing a personal crisis with access to 24hr crisis support and suicide prevention services.

Phone: 13 11 14

Beyond Blue provides information and support to help everyone in Australia achieve their best possible mental health, whatever their age and wherever they live.

Phone: 1300 224 636